7-13-76

# SLUMLORD!

# SLUMLORD!

The True Story of the Man
Who Is Beating
America's Biggest Problem

## ALBERT LEE

ARLINGTON HOUSE·PUBLISHERS
NEW ROCHELLE, NEW YORK

Manufactured in the United States of America

**Library of Congress Cataloging in Publication Data**

Lee, Albert, 1942–
  Slumlord!

  1.  Costa, Charles.  2.  Housing—Michigan—
Detroit.  3.  Slums—Michigan—Detroit.  I.  Title.
HD7304.D6L43        301.5'4'0924 [B]        76-4784
ISBN 0-87000-360-7

# Contents

1920813

# SLUMLORD!

# Author's Preface

Only a nonfiction novel could capture the bizarre true-life story of Charles Costa, the man they called "slumlord." I came to that conclusion after a year of studying this man and the slums he struggled in. I came to that conclusion after numerous meetings with the people who lived in the slums and with those who thrived or doted on them. What I discovered is that my notes did not contain words, rational analyses, or statistics, but pure, unadulterated emotions. I learned that the language of the slums is a muted tongue, a dialect of violence, of fear, and of misspent pity.

The story of the decay of our cities is an emotional narrative of people in turmoil. No amount of rhetoric can deal with the resentment and hatred which feed the slum violence. No statistics on the mass exodus from our cities can express the fear that drove them away. No bar chart can detail the compassion and guilt feelings which blur the vision of social workers, clergymen, judges, and legislators who unwittingly perpetuate the slums.

To survive the violence within the slums you must either become callous to human emotions and shield yourself with indifference, or you must learn the language of violence and meet the emotions head-on. Charles Costa chose to fight.

This book is the true story of Charles Costa's fight for his survival, for his family, for decent housing for the five thousand people in his buildings, and for the survival of the city he had adopted as his own.

9

The story is true. Every event actually happened. Every characterization within the covers of this book is real. Charles Costa's real name and the names of members of his family have been retained, while all other names have been changed. The events have been compressed, the chronology altered, and dialogue added—all to make the true story assume the form of a novel and thus retain the emotional impact that only such a narrative can convey.

This story is violent. To communicate the emotions of a cancer in the bowels of a city, the violence was necessarily included. I will not apologize for it here. But I will say that, if anything, the actual violence of Detroit's inner city and Charles Costa's part in it have been played down so as not to strain your concept of believability or to repulse your sensibilities. In real life, Costa's buildings averaged from two to three murders a month. Narcotics, prostitution, rape, child abuse, and all manner of cruelty and perversion were regular tenants in his dwellings. To portray all of this would have taken a new chapter for virtually every day of the ten years Costa has survived in his bizarre environment.

This story reaches beyond the city limits of Detroit. The problems Charles Costa faced are not unique to this one Midwestern factory town. According to the Census Bureau, the majority of our cities are losing their middle-class inhabitants. St. Louis has fallen in population back to 1890 census figures. Jersey City today hasn't been so empty since the turn of the century. Those left behind in our cities are faced with a crime rate that has quadrupled in less than a score of years, and the most recent national polls show that seventy-seven percent of all metropolitan women are afraid to walk out on the street in front of their homes at night. Afraid for good reason.

Charles Costa was never aware of these statistics. He was a man of action and emotion, not of numbers. Had he been given the statistics, he would have shrugged them off and continued to fight the system that preyed on his tenants and to substitute reason for violence. Perhaps that's what makes Charles Costa unique. That may be why his violent and tragic story contains a thin vein of hope for the future of our cities and our people.

*Southfield, Michigan*                                                    ALBERT LEE
      *October 7, 1975*

10

# 1

No one noticed the blood on the sidewalk. The blood formed a kidney-shaped pool with two arteries that had streamed into the sidewalk crack. More blood was spread like acne on the brown brick face of a gutted store nearby. No one noticed that either. People walked the sidewalk, some alongside the blood, some through it. They looked ahead, unmindful of the blood beneath their shuffling soles. Charles Costa walked in the same mid-morning crowd on Twelfth Street. He saw the blood, and stopped. Enough to drain a child, he thought, or send some john to Detroit General Hospital. Costa had seen blood on the sidewalk many times and, like the others who passed, he no longer speculated whose skull or belly spilled it, nor who made it happen. Those were last night's questions—today's was, why is it still here? A couple of years back, he thought, someone would have mopped the blood up, but now it would lie for days until the sun dried it and the winds drove it away.

"Hey, Jimmy," Costa yelled to a man standing next to a brownstone apartment building across the street. "Jimmy, get someone to clean up this mess."

Jimmy saw Costa and walked toward him. He walked slowly with arms hung limp. The man's hair stood up in uneven bristles, and Costa knew it represented an obvious failing grade at the barber college down the street. Jimmy's trousers were too large, bloused in at the waist by a thin belt. The trouser fly was half open.

"Come on, Jimmy," Costa said, "get this blood cleaned up. How come you're not looking out for me, man?"

"Yeah, well, ah . . . . ."

"Look, Jimmy, you're the manager of that building now," Costa said as he pointed to the brownstone Jimmy had come from. "It's your job to keep the street cleaned up, and keep those rummies off the porch. There are kids around here. You want them to see that crap?"

"Shit, Chuck. I don't know when every head gets busted. Shit. I just come downstairs, just then. I mean, I can't be watchin'—"

"OK, OK," Costa said. He placed a hand on Jimmy's shoulder. "After you get it up, I want you to do me a favor. Get Georgie, Jo-Jo, and the other cleanup guys. Tell them we got a new building to flood. Bring all the equipment, and some guns. But tell Jo-Jo not to bring that shotgun. He's always scaring the hell out of everyone with that thing. You tell them, pistols only. You hear?"

Jimmy bobbed his head in acknowledgment. "Sure, a flood."

"Go to it," Costa said. He smiled and backed away from Jimmy. "One more little thing. Quit advertising and zip up your pants."

Costa decided to walk the two blocks back to his office. The day was perfect for walking. The October air was cool and jagged sharp, and the wind drove the air into every pore on his face. The clouds, which were always solid over Detroit this time of year, were lower than usual, and Costa knew that sound carried better under them. He could hear the music in every building he passed. No song in particular. For the music came from every apartment—some acid rock, some soul sounds, some hillbilly spiked with the twang of a Hawaiian guitar. The various melodies mingled in the hall and poured into the street in a blur of noise. Sometimes a strain, a phrase, a melody came through, but mostly there were the low-bass vibrations, and the beat, constant and contagious. And the beat goes on, Costa thought as he rounded the corner and quickened his pace to get his step in tempo.

"Mr. Costa," a voice called out from behind him. He turned to see a black woman coming toward him. She was massive. Her arms were as big as hams, and under one of them she had two boys.

12

"Mr. Costa. You gotta help me, Mr. Costa. I need a place for my kids. My sister Abigail, she's in one of your buil'in's, and she says it's clean and all. And she says, 'You go talk to Mr. Costa. He'll find you a place, Lucy!'"

"Abigail?" Costa said. "You mean Abigail Johnson at 1468 Henry? Yes, I remember her. From Alabama, isn't she?"

"Yes, Mr. Costa. And so am I. The kids and me, we came up 'cause Abigail called and said things were fine in Detroit. Well, they ain't been."

"No?" Costa said, as he continued to walk, steering the woman in the same direction.

"Not at all fine, Mr. Costa. Look here at my boy Martin Luther." She ejected the tallest child out from under her arm with a thrust that Costa was sure would knock the boy down, but he stayed on his feet. She grabbed the boy by the head, bent it over, and exposed a neck with a patch of flesh missing. "That's what the rats did in that place, Mr. Costa. The place is loaded with rats. They bit Martin Luther when he was sleeping on the couch. Just came up and bit him like he was supper. That's the kind of place we was living in, with rats that want to make eats of your children."

Costa stopped and looked at the boy's neck. "Has a doctor seen this? When did it happen, anyway?"

"Last week. I took the boys and moved out right then that night. I wasn't going to live in no house with rats. They liked to eat Martin Luther up."

The wound on the boy's neck looked swollen to Costa. "Mrs. Johnson—is that your name?"

"Brown, Lucy Brown."

"Mrs. Brown, there's a public health clinic down on Randolph and Beaubien. I want you to take Martin Luther there right now. They won't charge you anything for treating the boy. Then you come back to my office up the street there and you tell Marilyn—she's my secretary—you tell her I said to fix you up in the new John R. building tomorrow. She'll take care of your paperwork with the welfare and fix you up good."

"No rats, is there, in your building?"

"Not in my buildings. I get them killed off, regular. But I want you to take care of the boy before we get you moved in." Costa looked down

13

at the boy. He looked frightened. "Don't worry, Martin, the people at the clinic won't hurt you." Costa took another look at the boy's neck, gripped his shoulder firmly, then pointed him and his mother in the direction of the health clinic.

Costa hurried the rest of the way to his office. He walked hard. His heels struck with force enough to practically dig themselves into the brittle pavement. As he passed, people yelled to him from porches, windows, and archways. He waved and smiled back without slackening his stride. He came on his office in a near run, skipping two steps at a time onto the porch. The office was a house, an upright two-story with fresh blue paint covering, yet not concealing, the scrolled wood framing that dated its construction to the pre-World War I era. The heavy oak door banged shut behind him. One step within and Costa stood in a modern office. The ceiling was low and lit from within with diffuse fluorescent lights. The walls were paneled. The reception room chairs were dabs of color and contemporary design. Half a dozen men occupied the chairs. Their clothes were dingy, their chins unshaven, their expressions stern. Even Costa, who was used to the scene, couldn't help noticing at times how these building managers, in to pay rents, contradicted the décor of his office as surely as the office itself clashed with the house that enveloped it. But today he had no time to notice. He walked into the middle of the room, glanced around in a sliding nod of recognition, then slipped into his inner office.

Marilyn was on the telephone talking, as best as Costa could figure out, to someone from one of the social agencies who was trying to place a couple of welfare families. The telephone receiver appeared huge alongside of Marilyn's head. Little Merl, Costa sometimes called her. She was petite, yet with olive skin and dark eyes like his own, which made her seem sturdier than her slight build indicated. Costa picked up the stack of phone messages from the desk in front of Marilyn and looked through them until she got off the telephone.

"Merl, call the newspapers. Tell them that Chuck Costa is putting a bounty on rats. I'll pay a dime a head—no, twenty cents each for, say, twenty-five hundred rats. And I'll challenge other landlords to do the same." As Costa talked, he reached under the desk top and pulled out his .38-caliber snub-nosed revolver. He checked the chambers to be

14

certain it was fully loaded, then slipped the gun under his belt behind his back and pulled his heavy wool sweater back down over the bulge. "Tell them to put my rat bounty in the paper right away."

Marilyn wrote down his directions without expressing visible surprise at either the instructions or his gun play. She had worked for Costa one year—long enough that nothing he did could wrinkle an eyebrow.

"Where do you want the rats delivered, and who should pay for them?"

"Have them come here. Tell Billy to come over here to receive them and pay for them. Put them in plastic bags, big bags. Then have someone else recount Billy's tally and take them to the dump."

"All right," Marilyn said. "Did you see the messages from your lawyer? He's called three times this morning and says he has to talk to you. He said something about a new law passing in the state capitol that could create a lot of trouble. I didn't get the whole message because the other phones were ringing, but I think it's serious."

"Ralph's a worrier. All we got is trouble down here. One more do-gooder law can't screw it up much more."

"He sounded upset," Marilyn said, "a lot more than he usually is. I think it's important."

"Not now. I've got a building to flood, and it's a bad one. If Ralph calls again, tell him to come over here later." Costa headed for the door, then turned around. "Almost forgot. A welfare gal with two kids will be by. Her name's Lucy Brown. Put her in 650 John R., in that back three-bedroom. It will be ready tomorrow. But before you send her over, check her boy Martin. Make sure the kid's neck was bandaged up at the health clinic. If it isn't, you send that woman to the clinic. You tell her Costa said, no treatment for the kid, no apartment."

Outside, Costa walked to the garage on the back of his lot. The garage leaned slightly to the alley side. It was a one-car structure, an afterthought for a house built before motorcars came into vogue. He opened the rickety wooden doors, revealing a white Cadillac Eldorado, a car of such grand scale that it looked like the garage must have been built around it and would have to be chopped away to remove the car. But, walking sideways, Costa slipped into the garage and managed to drive the car out unscathed.

15

Georgie and the crew pulled up in the alley behind Costa's Cadillac. In the rearview mirror Costa could see that Georgie had five men with him—two crowded in with Georgie in the cab of the pickup truck and three more hanging onto the rusted sides of the truck bed. Two ladders were tied on the truck racks with strands of electrical wire. The truck's front bumper sagged on the right side, and with its sun-bleached red hood and dented fenders, Costa personified the vehicle as an old wino staggering along in unsteady search for a gutter to lie in.

Georgie got out of the truck and walked up to Costa's Cadillac, bending like a jackknife at the middle to lower his tall torso enough to peer in at Costa.

*"Cali mera ti kanis, Costa. Pou pigenis?"*

*"Pao stin thoulia,"* Chuck answered. He reached out the window and patted the top of Georgie's black hair. Costa liked Georgie's spunk, and he delighted in Georgie's insistence on speaking Greek most of the time. Costa could speak several languages beyond his native Maltese, but Greek wasn't his strongest one, so he enjoyed practicing it whenever Georgie came to work for him.

They babbled in Greek over the car windowsill until the roar of an approaching motorcycle drowned them out. The cycle pulled up alongside Costa's car. It was a custom bike, with a seat so low and handlebars and sissy bars so high that it stood like a swayback horse. On it rode Jo-Jo, a man so large as to dwarf the machine he rode on. Costa had known Jo-Jo for upwards of a decade, and he never quite got used to the man's bigness, nor his grizzliness—three hundred pounds in Levi's and mackinaw shirt with a black leather vest and wide belt topping his cyclist regalia. Costa figured Jo-Jo to be at least six feet four, a full head taller than himself. He was broad-shouldered enough to impress Chuck, who considered himself fairly husky. And Jo-Jo's face was even more imposing, pockmarked with a single thick eyebrow that ran unbroken across the width of his brow. Jo-Jo was a deaf-mute, and the unnerving silence of the man reinforced his repugnancy. Costa had taken Jo-Jo into many a tough situation and knew him to be as formidable as he appeared, yet Costa also knew that he was as soft as mush inside and as loyal as a spinster's toy Chihuahua.

Costa raised both hands in front of him, and his fingers began

16

dancing in the language of the deaf. Jo-Jo smiled and answered with his own thick fingers.

Costa looked to Georgie. "Jo-Jo says he didn't bring the shotgun because he figured I'd bust it over his head this time for sure," Chuck said, laughing more visibly than normal to let Jo-Jo know he was pleased. Chuck told Jo-Jo in sign language to follow and told Georgie in Greek to follow, and then the odd caravan of Cadillac, pickup truck, and motorcycle was underway.

Less than two miles later the caravan stopped on John R. Street in front of a five-story brick building. The street was quiet. Men stood in clumps on the corners and porches glaring at Chuck's crew. Those who recognized Chuck whispered to the others that there was going to be some action. Chuck got out of his car, Georgie and Jo-Jo joined him, and the five men grabbed toolboxes, paint cans, and rolls of electrical wiring. Those who were street-wise saw the bulges under the coats and sweaters of all eight men. Chuck started toward the door and the others followed, and the gallery of onlookers turned silent. A horn was blasting down the street, and it halted Costa and his procession on the steps. Chuck saw the car coming, a dark green Mercedes he recognized as belonging to Dr. Jewell. The doctor was waving toward Chuck and laying on his horn as he pulled up at the curb.

"Mr. Costa," the doctor called out. "Please, I want to talk to you."

Chuck was annoyed at the interruption, but he walked over to Jewell's car and manufactured a smile. "Hi, Doc. Come to see me take over your building?"

"I'm glad I caught you in time. I don't want to sell you this building. Look, I'll give you your check back." The doctor pulled out a piece of paper and pushed it toward Chuck.

"Deal's made, Doc. You signed the papers yesterday. What happened? You discover oil in the basement today?"

"Costa, I couldn't sleep last night thinking about being responsible for your death. I wasn't completely truthful with you. I left out a few things about this building that you should have known before you agreed to buy. I just can't do it to you. Someone will be injured, and I'll be responsible. I don't want anyone killed."

Chuck's forced grin became genuine and broad. "You're a surgeon,

17

you told me. Would a surgeon operate on a patient without first examining every nook and crevice on his body?''

''No.''

''Well, Doctor, I'm kind of a surgeon, too, only I operate on sick buildings and make them well. I'm not so unprofessional that I'd take a patient without doing some pokin' around. I know that this place is a shooting gallery with hopheads behind damn near every door.''

''But there have been killings here.''

''Yes, three people were shot this month, and I heard one of them was killed. It's a tough building, Doctor, and it's on the poorest street in town. Why, these people are so tough and poor that they wear hand-me-down bandages.''

''You should joke when you're about to walk into a narcotics den? I don't see anything amusing about these people.''

''No, I guess you don't,'' Chuck said, his smile disappearing. ''You professional people buy these buildings to make some serious money; then, when a street turns mean, you get serious scared. You don't come around any more because they don't pay easy, so the place falls apart. Then with a straight face you sucker some dude like me into taking it off your hands. Someone else is left to clean up your mess or take the loss when the place crumbles. That's damn serious business.''

''Take your check back, please, Mr. Costa. I'll have the building boarded up so no one will get hurt.''

''Sorry, Doc. We made a firm deal. You were satisfied with the price yesterday; so was I. We had two smiles, and that's what a deal should be,'' Chuck said. He began walking toward the building. ''I'm going to flood it with repair people, and wash out your dope-head tenants. If I let you have it back, the wrecking ball would have it in a few months. It's too sound a building for that.''

''All right,'' the doctor yelled, ''but remember, I'm not responsible.''

''I know you're not,'' Costa mumbled to himself as he crossed over the threshold.

The stairway was steep, narrow, and dark, lighted only by a grime-filmed window on each landing. The air was still, and Chuck could see the dust suspended in tubes of light. As he climbed the stairs, he ran his hand along the wallpaper. It was brittle to the touch, like parchment. The wallpaper pattern was a flowered urn, sallowed by age, marked with water, crayon, and bloodstains, and scored by sporadic gyres of chipped paper. Chuck couldn't resist picking off chunks of the chipped paper, any more than a child can leave a scab unpulled. Besides, he knew that if the flooding was successful, he would have the walls recovered, so another chip gone was of small consequence now.

He was climbing to the fourth and top floor and would work down with the flooding. Having had debris dropped on him from above before, he knew that a top-down approach was safer. As he climbed, Chuck made mental note of which apartments were occupied. It was easy to tell. If there were people, there was the beat, the bass notes, coming out over a transom here, another there. The music was loud —the walls vibrated in rhythm, yet in his fifteen years as an inner-city landlord, no one had ever complained about the noise. It was the sound of life here.

There were six doors on the fourth floor. Costa went to the last one, the one with music. Jo-Jo and Georgie followed. Costa had left the others in the lobby to wait. The halls were narrow; too many men would stumble over one another. Chuck stood alongside the door and motioned to Jo-Jo and Georgie to move out of direct line. Then he knocked hard. No answer. He knocked again. "Open up. It's your landlord."

"What's you want out there?"

"It's your new landlord," Chuck said. "Come to collect the rent."

The voice came back from behind the closed door: "Shag ass, man. We ain't got no rent. Get the f - - - out of here."

Chuck stepped back, and in one kick, sprung open the door. The heat struck Chuck in a suffocating wave as he stepped into the room. The radiators were wide open, he thought, as he walked fast to close the ten steps between the door and the man who had been yelling from behind it. He was a white man, stripped to the waist and sweating hard. Behind him on the couch was another man. He, too, was only half dressed.

19

"What's you doing, you motherf - - -?" the closest man said, as he backed up against the wall.

Chuck came within inches of the man's face. "I told you; I'm your landlord. I want to see your rent receipts."

"You got no rights busting in here . . . ." As the first man talked, the one on the couch got up, pulled a knife, and started for Chuck's back. Chuck heard Jo-Jo grunt a warning and turned in time to face the man. Chuck reached behind his sweater, pulled out the pistol, and in one swirling motion brought the barrel across the attacker's face. Chuck could hear the man's face crumple from the blow. He fell back onto the couch, holding his bloodied mouth. By this time both Jo-Jo and Georgie had their guns drawn and were pointing them at the first man, who was glued against the wall. Chuck walked back into the kitchen. The room was rancid with the smell of decaying food, left on tabletops and on the floor. Whiskey bottles and crunched cans completed the floor decorations. The other rooms were equally adorned with debris. In the bedroom he found a pistol and some women's jewelry in a bureau drawer. In the bathroom he saw the blood-speckled walls and tub where veins had squirted out from heroin injections. Next to the toilet lay the spent matches, spoon, and hypodermic syringe. Chuck brought the gun, jewelry and hypo into the front room.

"This stuff belong to you?" Chuck said. He held it out in front of the standing man. He didn't answer, not in words, but Chuck understood the piercing gaze to be answer enough. Chuck looked at the man on the couch. He was sitting up now, letting the blood flow out of his mouth without any interest in stopping it.

"Both of you get your clothes and get out. We'll wait," Chuck said. "Move!" The standing man reached out for the syringe. Chuck dropped it and stepped on it.

"Rotten mother," the man said, falling to his knees and picking up the needle and part of the plunger. "Somebody going to bust your ass wide open. Rotten mother."

Next door Chuck knocked again. "Yeah, man," a voice answered from the other side, "what's up?"

"It's your new landlord," Chuck said. "I want to talk to you."

20

The door opened and a young black man, decked out in a satin shirt with flared sleeves, tight trousers, and high-heeled boots, stood before him. The young man's entire outfit, including the shoes, was purple. "Hi. I just came around to see your rent receipt," Chuck said. "Can I come in?"

"Sure, but we ain't got no receipts," the young man said. He opened the door, and Chuck saw three more brightly outfitted men in the room. Chuck sized them up as hustlers of some kind—smooth talkers. He decided to play it their way.

"Hey, man," Chuck said, "tell you why I'm talking to you. This joint is done tore up, and I put my money in it. If I don't make it now man, hell, you know. I understand the police are gonna come around and bust every goddamn door in and haul everybody outta here because of the narcotics. Man, I don't want these doors busted any more than they are. I'd just as soon you'd leave." As Chuck talked, he rubbed his hand over the bulge in the sweater, making sure that his audience had no misconception of what was under it.

"Mind if I talk this out with my friends?" the young man asked.

"Not if you hurry. But you know man, them cops are going to be around damn soon."

The man went to the other side of the room with the other three, and Chuck could hear him whispering. "This crazy goddamned landlord's got a gun under that sweater."

"Did you see that big guy in the hall?" one of the others asked.

"If there's going to be fuzz, man, we ought to split. Besides, I don't trust that crazy bastard with the gun. He might just start shooting to save his doors."

"We're going, man," the young man said to Chuck. "We'll be out tomorrow."

"Cops are coming sooner than that," Chuck said. "Why don't you cut out now?"

"Ah, sure man. No trouble, we're going."

The rest of the rooms on the fourth floor were vacant. A couple had been vandalized with radiators missing and the sink pulled out of the walls; the rest were just dirty. Chuck had his five-man crew take over the

21

floor and start cleaning up as he, Jo-Jo, and Georgie went down to the third floor, the second, and finally the first. The few inhabitants they encountered, all male and all hopped-up or winding down from highs, left without a fight. Chuck came to the last door. There was no beat, no answer, yet the door was locked.

"Open up. It's your landlord," Chuck repeated, but no answer. He stepped back and raised his leg to kick in the door when he heard a lock bolt click. The door opened enough so that Chuck could see three night chains stretch and a portion of a wrinkled black face. "I'm Chuck Costa, ma'am, your new landlord. I just bought this building, and I want to talk to you."

The woman hesitated for a long moment, then closed the door, removed the chains, and opened the door about a foot.

"Here's my card," Chuck said. "Can I come in?"

She stared at the red printed card. It read: *Charles Costa–Better City Living–Buy-Sell-Rent.* She moved back, and Chuck entered, motioning for the others to stay in the hall. The woman looked up at Chuck from a face so furrowed that he could not detect expression. Her eyes were glazed, yet, Chuck thought, bright and aware.

"I wanted to pay my rent," she began, "but nobody came around. I would have paid my rent before this, but I couldn't leave. Those boys knocked me down last time I went out. They took my purse. I just couldn't leave out of here."

The words rushed out of her, stumbling, or leaping off into high-pitched cracks. It's fear talking, Chuck thought, and he let her go on and get it out of her system. When there were no more words left, the old woman sat down and cried, quietly at first, then in torrents. Chuck waited for her to get it all out. He got up, glancing around at the neat apartment, busy with plants, doilies, and dime-store pictures of puppies and big-eyed children.

"I'm sorry," she finally said. "It's just, I could hear them upstairs. All the time screamin' and fightin', and I couldn't go out, or they'd see me. I couldn't even wash, or they would hear my water and find me."

"I've thrown them all out," he said, quick to head off more tears. "We're cleaning up the building, and you'll have good neighbors. Until

22

then, my repair guys will be around twenty-four hours. They won't come back.''

She began crying, this time in sobs that Chuck thought sounded like a small, lost child. "I couldn't get no food," she said. "They would hit me if I went out. They did it before.''

"Georgie," Chuck called. "Come on in here. This is Mrs. . . . well, how about that? I don't even know this good lady's name.''

"Eloise," she said, juggling some wrinkles into a faint smile.

"Eloise, meet Georgie. He'll drive you to Kroger's and help you shop.'' Chuck pulled his wallet out and handed Georgie two twenty-dollar bills. "You can pay me back a little at a time from your checks, Eloise. And don't worry about back rent. The last landlord should have paid *you* for staying here.''

Though it was midafternoon when Chuck stepped out of the building, it was overcast, dark, and cold. Chuck sat on the steps alongside Jo-Jo. The icy cement penetrated through Chuck's Levi's and felt good on his legs and backside. Jo-Jo offered Chuck a Chesterfield. He leaned back and lit up, drawing hard to fill up on the soothing smoke. The flooding had gone better than most—no shooting, no ambulances. In a couple of days the place would be clean, painted, and filled with families. He thought of bringing the doctor back in a week or so to show him what he'd dumped. No, it would only encourage the man to buy more buildings, let them get out of hand, and maybe next time get himself sliced up. Chuck took another puff on the Chesterfield and let himself revel in a moment of smugness. Sure, I'm a slumlord, but I'm a damned good one. At that moment Chuck felt in complete control of his destiny, and he would have laughed at seers who could tell him otherwise. I can handle it, he thought. I can handle all of it.

"Chuck, Chuck," Jimmy called out as he approached. "Hey, Chuck.''

Chuck tossed the cigarette away and waited for Jimmy to deliver some problems. "What are you doing here?''

"Marilyn, she sent me. She said for you to come quick. There's a bunch of people out front of your house carrying signs.''

"Pickets?" Chuck beamed. "You've got to be kidding.''

23

"No shittin'. They're all over the place. Your lawyer's at the house. He says for you to come quick, is all. And you know that blood? I got it all mopped up."

"Blood? Oh, that. Good, Jimmy, you're doing good," Chuck said, then suddenly broke out laughing. "You know, Jimmy, the only difference between this business I'm in and a three-ring circus . . . is about two rings."

Jimmy stood bland-faced, obviously wondering what Chuck was talking about and what was so outrageously funny.

"Never mind, Jimmy," Chuck said, patting Jo-Jo a silent good-bye on the shoulder. "Come on, Jimmy, you can ride back to the circus with me."

# 2

The rain came in rapid volleys. The drops pelted the Cadillac and set up a muffled racket inside that drowned out the hum of the engine. The drops were white, nearly frozen, and they stuck to the windshield like spitballs. The wiper blades slapped, but that only smeared the drops out into glazed crescents. Chuck slowed down and strained to see between the milk-white streaks. Jimmy was asleep in the seat alongside him. The stagnant car heater and the cushioned seat had lulled Jimmy to sleep only minutes after they left the new building, and the tinny medley of raindrops did nothing to stir him.

Through the glazed windshield Chuck could see the picketers in front of his house. Wayne students, he concluded, and that was summation enough for him. For Chuck gave little recognition to Wayne State University students. The school was in the inner city, just a fifteen-minute protest march from his front door. It was a geographic blunder that gave the suburban students a look at the wailing, weeping, and hair pulling of poverty, yet not close enough, Chuck thought, to hear the dialogue. Pupils. To him they were more accurately irritants in the eye of the inner city.

There were eight protesters, mostly girls, walking hunched against the rain in an elliptical course in front of his front door. Everyone carried a sign with Magic Markered slogans that Costa thought lacked the imagination of bathroom graffiti. "Poor Power," one read, carried by a svelte blond girl in faded jeans and suede jacket with matching shoes and purse. "Slumlords Suck," was the message a long-haired boy in a wrinkled raincoat displayed. "Costa is a Capitalist Pig," read another decorated with swastikas. Only one of the signs was unreadable. The girl who carried it held it horizontally over her head to stave off the rain. Well, Chuck thought as he pulled into the driveway, there's at least one kid in the bunch with some common sense.

Chuck reached over and nudged Jimmy. "Hey, we're here," Chuck said. He paused to let him come around. "Jimmy, I want you to stay in the car for a while. Lock the doors after I get out and stay put. Listen to the radio or something."

The rain and the picketers rushed at Chuck as he stepped out of the car. Chuck raised his arms wide. "Please, let Mr. Costa get into his office," Chuck said, looking back over his shoulder at Jimmy sitting in the car. "Let Mr. Costa get out of his car."

The picketers pushed past Chuck and swarmed over the Cadillac. They cursed through the windows at Jimmy and tried the doors in vain. Jimmy just sat listlessly, threatening to go back to sleep despite the commotion.

Chuck went into the office. Ralph O'Hara was at the window when Chuck entered. O'Hara stood about a foot away from the windowpane, a space dictated by his bulging vest that rode up, not quite covering the shirt stretched tight over his belly.

"Those your friends?" Chuck asked as he greeted O'Hara with an outstretched hand.

"That's not *my* name on those placards, Chuck. It's you they'll be wanting to tear apart. But I've got to talk to you, and it's more important than that rabble."

"Let's get the kids off my car first, Ralph. They're keeping Jimmy awake. What do they want?"

"I heard their leader, that tall blond there banging the stick against your windshield. She was bantering on about some crippled old lady you booted out into the street. She was hot about it."

"Marilyn, come in here," Chuck shouted, then addressed O'Hara

26

again. "It's got to be a mix-up. You know my open-door policy. I let anyone into my buildings, and I don't toss old ladies out."

O'Hara shrugged. Marilyn entered, as usual, carrying a stack of telephone messages.

"What's going on here?" Chuck said. He smiled to show Marilyn and Ralph that he was more amused than wrangled. "I've only been gone a couple of hours, Marilyn, and you've let the place go to pot."

"They're from Wayne," Marilyn said. "One of them—Susan Stanicki, I think she said her name was—says they're protesting your treatment of Matty Fuller."

"Isn't she the one you wanted me to process eviction papers on last week?" O'Hara asked.

"She sure is," Chuck said. He walked over to the window and opened it. "Hey, kids, get off of that car. I'm Chuck Costa, here. Come on in out of the rain and have some coffee."

Marilyn scurried out of the room to find cups for the bunch as they came in mumbling, still holding fast to their picket signs. They mulled a minute, then sat on the floor, ignoring the dozen chairs that lined both sides of the outer office. The blond girl whispered to the others, stood up, and approached Chuck and Ralph, who were sitting on the edge of the receptionist's desk. She was wet clear through, Chuck thought, and she had a look that blamed it all on him.

"Mr. Costa," she said. She stared right at Ralph O'Hara.

"No, ma'am. He's the one you want."

"Mr. Costa. How dare you give Mrs. Fuller notice to move. How can you use your power over the poor that way? We demand—"

"Hold it right there, young lady," Chuck said, getting up. "Guests in my house ask, they don't demand. Now let me tell you about poor Matty Fuller. She came to me three months ago with three kids. When she moved in, I found she had *six* kids, three dogs, and a sly husband sniffing around at night so Matty wouldn't lose her Aid to Dependent Children checks."

"She has to live somewhere," Susan broke in.

"That's what I said, so I let her stay in that building, even though she lied to me. But then came the trouble. Her kids beat up on every other kid in the building, and one of them shit in the hall and smeared it on the

27

walls. Sweet Matty Fuller sicced her three dogs on other tenants, and she's done more damage to the place than her rent can cover.''

"That's your side of it," Susan said. "I don't believe you.''

"Don't believe me. Go ask the tenants, ask the building manager, ask the police who've come out five or six times on complaints about her. Miss Stanicki, I have a responsibility to all of the tenants in a building, and I can't let people like Matty ruin things.''

"We don't believe you. We want that crippled lady to keep her apartment. You should apologize for picking on these poor people and taking their rent money.''

"How do you think I could stay in business without collecting rents? My rents are low, you ask anyone. And I give my tenants a clean, safe place to live. If I have to get rid of a Matty Fuller to do it, that's too bad. Jesus Christ.''

"Don't swear at me, slumlord," Susan said. Chuck saw her fists clench. She was losing the argument in front of her following. He'd have to bolster her up or she couldn't back down.

"OK, Miss Stanicki, we're not getting anywhere with this. You're right to stand up for the poor. I respect that. I think you have bad information about Matty Fuller, but I don't want to be unreasonable.'' Merl walked in as Chuck talked. She slipped a message into his hand. He read the message and shook his head. "Look, I've got other things to do, so I want to settle this mess now. I've got a little house on the same street as the apartment Matty lives in. Seven rooms. I'll move her in there at eighty-five dollars a month, the same as ADC is now paying for her apartment.''

Susan looked around at the others for reactions. They all seemed surprised. She turned back to face Costa with a similar uncertain expression.

"Hey," Chuck said. "You sit down and talk it over. Have some coffee and warm up. I've got an emergency to attend to.'' Chuck held up the note as evidence. He went into his inner office with Ralph right behind him.

"Ralph, I've had an accident in my Cass Avenue Hotel. You know, the one I keep for drunks. I've got to make one call on it. Mind?''

Ralph shrugged and flopped into a chair while Chuck made his call.

After a three-minute lopsided conversation Chuck put down the receiver and laughed.

"I think I've seen too much of this crap," Chuck said. "It's beginning to warp my sense of humor. My manager just told me what happened. Some drunk on the third floor was tired of waiting for the elevator, so he took off his shoe, beat out the window in the elevator door, then stuck his head in, and looked up to see if the elevator was coming."

"And it came."

"Uh-huh," Chuck said. "What a mess. But for some reason the image of the stupid drunk sticking his head in there strikes me funny. I tell you, it's sick."

"Gallows humor," Ralph said. "You see so many deaths, so much violence, it loses shock value. Now, can I tell you why I came?" The telephone rang, and Ralph beat Chuck to it. "He's in conference," he said into the receiver, then set it down off the hook. "This is too important to have any more interruptions."

"All right," Chuck said. He leaned back in his chair and propped his feet up on the desk. "Let's hear it."

"Chuck, I've known you for, what, ten years? When I met you, you were selling eggs out of the trunk of your car and driving a pop truck to pay your rent. I knew you when you were singing in the strip joints and hustling on the pool tables. Now you're a big shot with, what, seventy-five buildings housing five thousand people."

"Something like that," Chuck said, "but get on with it, Ralph; I've got things to do."

"Sit still for a minute. This is important. They've passed a law in the state capitol that's going to destroy you, and all you can do is run around buying buildings and getting yourself in deeper. It's time to get out, dump everything while you can."

"What are you talking about?"

"The Welfare Reform Bill. It has one provision that all public aid monies will go directly to the recipient. The tenants will get their money instead of the rent portion coming to you. Almost every one of your tenants is on public assistance. If they get their money directly and can't pay, you'll go under."

29

"Why the change?"

"It's an election year. Some politicians say welfare people should make their own decisions about spending their welfare checks. It's degrading to have bills paid for them as if they were children. It's supposed to give them more responsibility, or whatever."

"I treat my tenants well. They'll pay their rents."

"You don't really believe they'll pay, Charles?"

"No, I guess not, but if they don't, we can get rid of them."

"You can't evict all five thousand families. I warned you before not to take on so many hardship cases. Besides, you don't have any money to survive. It would take months to throw out all of the welfare types and find working people. I've warned you not to move so fast. You take every cent that comes in and buy more buildings. Nothing put away at all. You don't have any security."

"I'm beating the demolition ball. Landlords are abandoning this city, Ralph. They're running scared, and they're willing to practically give buildings away to get out with their skins. I'm the only one who can make those buildings come back. What you want me to do is throw away my business and abandon my people. Make some sense. I mean, it's good business to buy valuable property cheap."

"And sell it high," Ralph said. "You've fixed those buildings up, and you could make a profit on them and get out before the new law becomes binding."

Chuck got up and walked over to the window. The sky was black. Streetlights were on, and every house and apartment on Lincoln Street was aglow. The houses and apartments all were on lots no wider than the buildings themselves, so forced together that the narrow beams of light from one window interconnected with the light from the next window, forming a string of glitter that was redolent of a diamond tiara. Chuck knew that it was an illusion. Each window was isolated from its neighbors. Nothing, not light, and certainly not people, reached out to touch one another.

"Ralph, stop worrying. If the new law comes, we'll figure out a way to live with it. We'll get it changed. I've lived through do-gooders screwing things up before."

"Be reasonable," Ralph said. He joined Chuck at the window. "I've always said you are going to get killed dealing with these people, but at least it looked like you might leave Anita a rich widow. There won't be any profit. It's going to destroy you, Chuck, and your wife and kids will be left with nothing."

"If that's the case, you had better collect your fees in advance. How about coming back for some supper as partial payment?"

"Sure, 'n' when have I ever gotten any kind of payment out of you besides one of your wife's meals? But I can't tonight. I've got to get on and see some paying customers. Seriously, Chuck. I've got a gut feeling about this whole business. It's telling me you'd better get out while you can. There's no profit in owning a bankrupt city and even less in getting your head blown off. This city has the highest murder rate in the country, and every day it gets worse. I'm telling you as a friend, I've got a bad gut feeling about all of it."

Chuck slapped Ralph across the belly. "Ralph, I don't know of anyone better equipped to get 'gut feelings' than you are, but this time I'd say it's just gas."

"You don't worry, I take it? Why, you're just thirty-five years old, Chuck, and your hair is stone white. Doesn't that tell you something about the kind of business you're in?"

"No. It says I'm my father's son. He ran an import business in Malta when I was a kid—a quiet business, but his hair was gray at thirty-five. Gray's in the genes, Ralph, not in the job."

"You're incorrigible," Ralph said. He began to walk out. "You're asking for a thrashing," he said, and left the office. The phone rang, and Chuck answered it.


About nine o'clock Chuck switched off the lights in his office and walked out the front door. He liked to lock up and leave by the front door, then walk around and enter the house by the back door. There was no reason to do it that way, for a door in his office opened directly into his home. But going outside was a break, a definite separation between office and home. It gave him a minute to catch his breath and mentally

31

transport himself from business to family life, just as a deep-sea diver comes up via a decompression chamber so that sudden change in pressures won't bring on the bends.

Buster, the family German shepherd, was barking from the basement as Chuck climbed the four steep back steps and entered the kitchen. Anita was sitting at the kitchen table, her crochet work spread partly over the Formica tabletop and partly across her knees. She looked up at Chuck for only a moment, then returned her eyes to the red yarn entwined through her fingers. Chuck knew the look and remembered that they had parted in an argument that morning and assumed she still had some pouting left in her.

"Kids in bed?" he asked as he walked over to the stove to turn on the gas jet under the teakettle.

"All except Pam. She's watching television," Anita said without looking up. A long silence ensued as Chuck stood by the sink until the water boiled and made his black tea in a thick restaurant coffee mug with a chip on the edge. He sat down at the table.

"Hey, you remember me telling you about that black minister last week?" Chuck said. "You know, the one who hit me up for a hundred and fifty dollars to get his storefront church going? Well, he skipped town. I got the canceled check back today. It was endorsed by a used-car lot. See? I can be conned, too."

Chuck paused, but Anita didn't respond. Christ, he thought, why won't she look me in the eye when she's pouting? He already knew the answer, of course. If she looked at him, she might start crying again. Anita was strong. She had to be, to take care of their five children in this neighborhood, but her soft blue eyes were given to tears. He knew her tear ducts would erupt at the drop of an adjective.

"It wasn't a total loss, about the preacher. He told me a darned good joke while he was buttering me up, about this bum who asks a passerby for twenty dollars and fifteen cents for a cup of coffee. 'But it only costs fifteen cents for coffee.' 'I know,' says the bum, 'but drinking coffee always makes me feel sexy' . . . . Come on, Anita, that joke cost me a hundred and fifty dollars. You could snicker at it, at least."

"Chuck, I think we've got to move out of here."

32

"We went all through that this morning, 'Nit. I told you I'd think about it."

"No, we've got to do it. The kids can't even play outside anymore. I can't even walk to the corner. Even Buster can't go outside."

"How's Buster?" Chuck asked. It was the dog that had precipitated the argument this morning. One of the neighborhood kids had sliced him across the nose, fourteen stitches worth. The dog had been inside the chain-link fence, but that didn't stop the boy from reaching across to cut Buster. The incident occurred a week ago. Buster hadn't recovered. The flesh was healing, but the dog was left with a deep prejudice against black children. They had stoned him many times, jabbed him with sticks, and tried to burn him with flaming books of matches. Each attack changed the dog. He became slightly more morose, more suspicious with every abuse. The cut nose completed the change, and now Buster was prejudiced. He'd lurch at the steel fence at every black person who walked by, striking the fence with force enough to send a tremor into the house. Chuck knew that Buster was dangerous and insisted that he be kept in the basement. That sparked the fuse to the argument about leaving the neighborhood.

"It's not Buster," Anita said. "We can get another dog. But our children. Pam has been pushed down and her lunch money taken a dozen times. She's afraid to go to school. And the others. I can't let the kids out in our backyard. Those people hate us, Chuck. It's not like before the riot. They really hate us now. They call our children honkies and gang up on them."

"You know better than that, 'Nit. Most of those neighbors are our friends."

"Not the young ones. They stare when we go down the street. It's a mean stare, like we did something to them. I'm scared for the kids."

"And you don't think I am? We've been all over this, 'Nit. My work is here. I can't move out to suburbia and leave my buildings. Christ, I've been raving about absentee landlords for years; I can't be one."

"Then sell the buildings. You could buy some business out of Detroit. You can succeed in anything you try, Chuck. Remember when we moved out to the farm? You didn't know which end of the cow to

33

milk, but in two years you were the best farmer in the county. Everyone was coming to you for advice on crops and feeding.''

"And my back gave out from the fourteen-hour days,'' Chuck added; but, like Anita, he recalled the good times on the farm—two fine years working with clean dirt and uncluttered lives, where the only pollution to consider was a manure pile. When things got rough, he too looked back to those days, but this wasn't the time to admit it.

"We wouldn't have to go to farming,'' Anita said. "There are other things, safer things. If you'd sell the buildings, you could do anything you wanted, and the kids could go to a decent school.''

"You and Ralph ought to get together. You'd do a fine duet.''

Chuck went upstairs to truncate the fight. The hallway was dark, but Chuck knew by braille where every doorknob was. That was one of the beauties of living in the same house for several years: It became as familiar as old shoes worn to every nonconformity of the flesh. There was no need to think about the place. It simply was. He opened the first door and looked in. Just enough streetlight edged in under the venetian blinds for Chuck to see the bunk beds where his eldest boys, Mario and Tony, slept. Across the room was the crib, the side down, where his Pepe slept. Pepe was nearly four years old, too old for a crib, but they hadn't gotten around to buying a bed yet, which was just fine with Pepe. He liked climbing in and out over the high sides and sleeping with his hands and feet hanging through the bars. Next door Chuck looked into the girls' room. Gina was turning in her sleep; Pam's bed was empty. He went in his own room, pulled off his turtleneck sweater, kicked off his shoes, then put the gun away in the top drawer.

Back downstairs, Chuck considered going back into the kitchen but thought better of it. Instead he entered the living room. It was dark except for the glow of a multicolored TV screen against the far wall. Pam sat, Buddha-fashion, on the floor in front of the tube, the light haloing the tangled outer strands of her shoulder-length hair. Pam was the eldest, a position that gave her prerogatives of seniority even at thirteen, one of which, later hours, she was now exercising. Chuck sat on the couch and flicked on the pole lamp. "Hi, Dad,'' she said, flipping the phrase over her shoulder like a bus driver announcing the next stop.

"Hi, Honey. Good show?''

34

"Yeah."

Chuck smiled at her back. Kids are flexible, he thought. Yesterday the world was coming unglued because of some toughs. Today, there she sits, oblivious to everything except Walt Disney's animated creatures. Still, Chuck was bothered. Pam was a pretty girl, with her mother's eyes and a figure that had begun to soften and round noticeably. Anita was right in a way, he thought. This was no place for a young woman, or toddlers, or even a dog. Chuck knew it, yet there was the hope. The city would come back. It had to, or . . . . He didn't want to entertain the alternatives. A riot. That would be pleasant compared to what would come. Chuck had lived the fiasco of the riot two years ago—forty-two dead officially, a hundred more missing by hearsay. Buildings were smashed, burned all around him, yet his property had been spared. His friends of the street had scratched, chalked, or painted "Soul Brother" on every one of his apartment buildings like the lamb's blood on Moses' door, and the violence passed over. The riot had been madness. There were shots from rooftops, cries of pain from the streets; yet there was laughter and there was fellowship. Blacks and whites helped each other through shattered store windows. Welfare grandmothers and street urchins shared the loot from the corner candy store. Bedlam, thus confined, turned on itself. Chuck remembered watching from the kitchen window, watching his neighbors on Lincoln loot the furniture warehouse on the back side of his alley. They cleaned house that night, burning their own shabby chairs, couches, and televisions in the street and replacing the old with store-fresh stuff. Two days later the police came with a van. Door to door they went, repossessing the stolen property. His neighbors were left with bare rooms. The rest of the riot went much the same way. Mobs set torches to stores and, armored by the flames, stood off firemen with volleys of bricks. The flames leaped the six-foot separations between stores and rows of homes, and the flames burned the rioters' homes out. All lost—razed houses, no place to buy essentials, and neighbors who made an exodus from the city. Chuck had screamed about the insanity, the self-feeding fear. He had implored people to stay. He encouraged those who had left to come back. Now was he to join them in exile from Detroit? Chuck didn't want to consider it—at least not tonight.

The back doorbell rang, and Chuck listened as Anita answered it, then a moment later entered the living room. She carried the *Free Press*. It was Detroit's morning paper, the city edition which came off the presses at ten P.M. Chuck had a special arrangement with one of the newspaper teamsters to drop the first paper at the house as soon as it came out. Often the inside pages would still be warm from the presses, a heat, Chuck figured, that lasted for about an hour. Anita also carried the semblance of a smile, betrayed by the redness of her eyes. She had been crying. She does that a lot lately, he thought, but it's done now, and she'll feel better. After fifteen years of living with this woman, Chuck believed he was as familiar with the patterns of her moods as he was with every faded freckle across her tip-turned nose. The wisp of a smile said she was through pouting. The way she carried the newspaper, cradled to her bosom like a child, said she wanted to end the emotional rift then.

"Pam," Anita said, after she placed the paper on Chuck's lap, "isn't it bed time?"

"Aw, Mom. It's still early."

"You heard your mother," Chuck said, speaking as softly as he could to assure Pam he meant not to scold. Pam came over and sat on Chuck's lap. The newspaper crumpled under her. Chuck hated a mussed paper. It made him want to cringe. He didn't, for fear it would be taken as rejection by Pam. "Give me a kiss, then get to bed. Tomorrow night I'll be done earlier, and we'll have some time to talk."

Pam obeyed, leaving Anita and Chuck alone. Anita sat alongside him on the couch. She had come to sit by him so many times after the kids were in bed that there was an impression in the plastic couch fabric awaiting her. She asked how the day went, then lay her head on the backrest to listen. Chuck recounted the high points, the rat bounty he'd decided on, the new building, and the teenage protesters swarming over old Jim and the Cadillac. He omitted the day's violence, the threats of violence, and Ralph's warnings, because he wanted to spare himself the reliving as much as he wanted to shelter her. As Chuck talked, he scanned the real estate columns of the newspaper, looking always for new buildings to buy. Infrequently a word in an ad would indicate that this might be one for him. He'd stop talking, read the ad more carefully, then circle it for an A.M. call. He repeated the process with other columns as well. FURNITURE FOR SALE, APPLIANCES, OFFICE EQUIPMENT, MISCELLANEOUS and TRADES, all were ferreted through as he talked. If there was any break in the routine, it came as a telephone call, and these came often enough at all hours to become routine, too. Somehow, completion of Chuck's stories coincided precisely with completion of his paper scanning. There would be a span of silence, some serious conversation, and bed. But tonight the quiet minute lingered, and Anita made no move to rise from the couch and end it.

"Chuck, I'm sorry. I know how much this city means to you. It's just that . . . well, I've had this feeling that something was about to happen."

"Like what?"

"I don't know, not exactly. It's just a sick feeling about, about what's happening here. I don't understand what's going on. I love this house and don't want to leave. But here lately . . . . Oh, I don't know."

"'Nit, things are better now than they've ever been for us. Remember when we had nothing to eat but a bunch of green bananas? Three days on that banana diet before I made enough money to buy some food."

Anita raised her upper lip. "Don't remind me," she said. "I still can't look at a banana without getting a little nauseated."

"We'll never get any worse off than we were back then. Now we've got all the buildings. You couldn't want more security. They stand there solid as the rock of St. Peter's Church, making money for us. I tell you, 'Nit, you're going to be a wealthy woman soon."

"As long as we don't go back to bananas, I don't care about money. I want both you and the children to be happy, that's all," Anita said. She looked away from Chuck and up at the ceiling. "I only hope both are possible here."

# 3

Had he told anyone to stand guard on the new building? Chuck wasn't sure. The uncertainty kept him fighting sleep. He tossed from side to side, his body restless for comfort, yet his mind grasping at hazy recollections of telling Georgie or Jo-Jo or one of the others to stay at the new place. But he couldn't remember, and the uncertainty drove him from bed. Chuck lit the last Chesterfield in the pack, got into Levi's and turtleneck sweater, slipped his pistol in his belt, and tossed on his suede jacket. He stopped in the bathroom only long enough to gargle and get a pack of cigarettes from the tub. The bathtub was filled with multicolored cigarette packs. Someone had busted open a cigarette machine in one of his hotels the night before, and though the machine had been ruined, Chuck managed to salvage most of its contents. He had never seen so many packs in one place; it was bizarre. Maybe he should load them into a dump truck, he mused, and he could dump the entire load on the next guy who approached him on the street to bum a smoke. Or perhaps he should donate the tobacco to the Michigan Cancer Foundation, in the same vein of righteousness as the little old ladies who had turned in their guns after the riots. Chuck toyed with a number of possibilities as foolish, he thought, as having a bathtub full of cigarettes in the first place. Finally, he ended his mental calisthenics, grabbed a pack, and left the house.

Chuck drove slowly down the side streets. They were covered with a cellophane-thin glaze where the afternoon rain and late evening chill had jelled. It was about two A.M., he estimated—a good time to drive down the action streets and get some entertainment on the way to the new building. He turned onto Third Street and immediately spied some action. Four whores, none much older than his own daughter, were arguing. Some man in a beige Chevrolet station wagon had stopped to pick one up. All four now hung on his open passenger door and were holding a screaming match to decide whose trick he was going to be. Chuck couldn't see the driver, but he imagined him as a teenager with daddy's car, fidgeting while the girls decided who was going to give him a case of clap to take back and share with his high-school friends.

Across the street in front of a bar five dudes huddled, talking bad about something. They wore wide-brimmed Superfly hats, bright jackets, patterned trousers, and three-inch high-heeled shoes. Chuck assumed they were hustlers—pimps maybe, muggers when the chance presented itself, murphy men if they could find a full john to pick. One of the men recognized Chuck's car and raised his clenched fist in a friendly salute of black power. Chuck motioned back and kept driving. With his dark Mediterranean features, wiry white hair, and brown eyes, many blacks assumed that Chuck was a soul brother, or at least a mulatto. Among blacks he spoke their language, just as he spoke Greek among the Greeks, Arabic among Egyptians, and Italian among Sicilians. Most weren't sure just what Chuck was, and he liked it fine that way. He liked being an ethnic chameleon. It was adaptation, and in this environment, adaptation meant survival. His Cadillac Eldorado was another adaptation for survival. Chuck dressed plain, Levi's and turtleneck, yet he wore the car as his raiment of success. He's one of us, they'd say. That dude came up from the street, and he's got a big hustle going. Some thought him a pimp, a Mafia chief, into numbers, a pusher. That was status here, and it earned the raised-fist salute of street camaraderie.

Costa parked his car two doors down from his building on John R. Street. He could see that none of his men's vehicles were around, and he had forgotten to assign a night watch on the place. Chuck thought of the old woman on the first floor and his promise to keep the dope heads out. As he approached the front steps, Chuck heard the bang coming from the second floor, a familiar sound of a pipe wrench against a radiator. He walked flat-footed around to the side of the house. The back was dark, but he could see the silhouette of a pickup truck in the alley. Chuck pulled out his gun and went back to the front porch. Someone was inside ripping off the plumbing, copper plumbing which would fetch a good price tomorrow in the junkyards. First he thought of finding a cop, but figured that might take an hour, and the strippers would be gone.

He went inside and followed the bang of metal against metal up the stairs. From the landing he could see the shadow of a man through the open door of an apartment. The man was tugging on a radiator, pulling it up onto the window ledge to drop it into the alley. But the awkward shape was giving him trouble, and the legs were catching on the ledge as he pulled. Costa stepped into the room. Out of the corner of his eye he saw a second shadow, this one coming down at him. A crowbar careened off Chuck's forehead and struck the gun in his hand, bouncing it across the room. The shadowed man pulled back the crowbar and lifted it high for a second blow. Chuck was dazed. He reached up and grabbed the man's arms. He stumbled, and they both fell on the floor. The man who had been at the window was now kicking at Chuck's side as he rolled with the other one. Chuck kept them rolling in the direction he assumed the gun had flown. The dust was thick, welling up and choking him as he rolled under and over the man with the crowbar, holding onto his arms with a cliff-hanger's grip. They rolled into the wall with Chuck on the bottom. He could feel the baseboard on one shoulder as he felt two hands grab his arm. There was something hard under his side. The gun, he thought, but he wasn't sure. To find out he had to let go of the man's arms, which would let him get a crack at him with the bar. But with the two of them on him, Chuck knew they would eventually break his grip, so the object was his only chance. He let go and reached for the lump under him. The man raised up with the crowbar and began to bring it down. But Chuck had the gun now, and he fired into the man's knee. The man dropped the crowbar and rolled off, holding his knee against his chest. Chuck got to his feet in time to see the second man running for the open door. "One more step. Go on, make it," Chuck yelled. The man stopped. "No, no, don't stop, you bastard. I want to blow your head off."

"I'm stopped. See? I ain't movin'. You ain't gonna kill me, man."

"Back up and help your buddy," Chuck said, feeling his own blood trickling down from his forehead. "Now, let's go downstairs and find a cop."

"Give us a hussle, man. Alls we did was take out some pipes. We'll put 'em back. We'll put 'em where we got 'em."

"How you gonna put 'em back?" Chuck said. "You ripped them out, tore up everything. You don't know how to build, just rip off."

It took several minutes to get the two men downstairs. The tall one carried his wounded friend like a basket of vegetables, repeatedly spilling him against the railing as he went down the stairs. Chuck was feeling whoozy, but he was clearheaded enough to keep his distance and keep the gun pointed in the right direction. As they stepped out onto the porch, Chuck was faced with a large group of people staring at him. The shot had evidently drawn them out to see some action.

"Hey, man, that dude got Raymond," one mingler yelled.

"Yeh, that's Raymond. Hey, Raymond, what's he doing to you?"

"Let Raymond go, you mother," some female voice said.

"You ain't taking him nowheres."

"Right on."

The chorus was rising, and Chuck knew the tune well—a crowd working its way up to be a mob. He had seen policemen beaten nearly to death trying to take a prisoner out of one of these buildings and running into a mob reaction. He knew something had to be done or he'd lose all control. Chuck pointed his gun just inches above the heads in the crowd and fired once, twice, three times. The crowd spread in every direction. "Move to that white Caddy, quick," he said to his prisoners, "or I'll use the rest of these shells on you."

Limping and stumbling, his prisoners got into the front seat of the Eldorado, and Chuck slipped in behind the wheel, then reached around and locked all the doors. The crowd hadn't gone far, and now it was reassembling around his car. He could hear threats being shouted, see teenagers throwing rocks, some running up and spitting on the car. They were in the road all around him. Chuck pulled out and drove through them at normal speed. They'll either move, or they won't, he thought. They moved aside.


Three hours later Chuck found himself at the counter of an all-night hamburger stand next to the police precinct office. The pair was booked, one into a cell, the other into the hospital security ward. All the complaint papers were signed, statements taken. Chuck's gun was taken—evidence, they had told him—his head was bandaged, and the shoulder of his suede jacket irrevocably stained with blood. He sat with his elbows on the counter, a cup of steaming tea nestled in his paws. Chuck was hazy from the lack of sleep and the pain in his head, but his stomach still churned from the adrenalin high. He had to calm down before he could go home.

"Excuse me. Are you Charles Costa?"

Chuck glanced up at the tall young man, then returned to sipping on his tea. "Right now, I'm not sure."

"Mr. Costa, I need your help. I've been calling your office for two days, and you haven't returned my call."

Chuck looked back at the man again. "I don't mean to be rude, but it's late, and I'm in no mood to talk. Why don't you call the office about a room?"

"It's not a room, sir. I need more help than that. I'm a landlord, like you. I've got a twenty-unit building, and it's gotten out of hand. Everyone says Charles Costa can help."

"It's five A.M. Have a heart. How did you find me here anyway? Don't you sleep?"

The man sat down next to Chuck. "I've been driving a cab the last couple weeks because of my building. Midnights. I was across the street talking to the desk sergeant when you were in there. Mr. Costa, I really have to have some help, or I'm going to lose my building."

The words surprised Chuck, not the words themselves, but the firmness in their utterance, a plea, yet one without groveling under-tones. Chuck looked at the cabdriver. There wasn't a hair on his head out of place, Chuck thought, even though the hair was blond and as wispy

43

as cobwebs. The hair was combed in a John Kennedy style, without oils, but not one hair was undisciplined.

"What makes you think I can help you? This bump on my head ought to say I'm not doing so well, taking care of Chuck Costa."

"Maybe you can't. Maybe my building's gone too far. Everyone says that you're the shrewdest landlord in this town. The police say they like you along on trouble calls because you thrive on tough stuff. Lots of guys have told me how you make impossible buildings pay. You taught Dave Karpinski how to operate buildings. He says—"

"Wait a minute. My head's throbbing, and I'm in no shape to talk business." Chuck got up and tossed two coins on the counter. "Tomorrow. You come around to my office tomorrow. We'll talk then. What's your name?"

"Peter Balantine," the cabby said. He stood up and extended his hand to Chuck. "Thank you, Mr. Costa."

"Sure. Balantine . . . are you any relation to . . . ." Chuck paused. "Forget it; I don't know what I'm doing. Small talk this time of the morning. I'll see you tomorrow."


By midafternoon Chuck was back at his office desk and on the telephone. Calls were his stock-in-trade. On days like yesterday when action came in buckets, the telephone messages stacked up. They had to be answered; and today, with his legs still wobbly from last night, was the perfect time. There were calls from people in need of shelter, calls from landlords offering "bargain" buildings for sale, and calls from his building managers about fights, fires, broken water pipes, and furnaces that had taken up smoking. Should the telephone not ring for five minutes, Chuck would pick up the receiver and start calling city councilmen about needed legislation, or real-estate agents, reminding them he was in the market for buildings, or managers to see what kinds of problems were detaining them from calling in their problems. The telephone was fast, efficient. It suited Costa's style. He enjoyed making the rounds of his buildings, gossiping with tenants and greasing his hands on a repair job, but that was his recreation; telephone contacts were his business. Today the calls were routine, and he was beginning to get restless with them, until his lawyer called.

"Chuck, you've done it again."

"What are you talking about?"

"You placed a reward on the recovery of dead rats. The announcement was in this morning's paper. How come you didn't tell me about it first?"

"Because it didn't take a lawyer, Ralph. The rat bounty was simple. You kill 'em, I'll pay for 'em. Don't tell me rats are considered an endangered species and I'm in trouble with the Society for the Prevention of Cruelty to Animals?"

"Worse. I have a Mrs. Olivia Benneditti in my outer office threatening to sue you for everything you've got, which we both know isn't much."

"Over rats?"

"Did you see the article? Did you read it, Chuck?"

"Sure. It was on page two. They even spelled my name right this time."

"Well, they got the address wrong. It says in the paper you'll pay twenty cents a rat when delivered to 26540 *Linden*. That happens to be the address of Olivia's Beauty Salon. A number of people have come to her door carrying garbage bags filled with rats. They refuse to leave until they've been paid. The lady is hysterical. Several of her customers ran out of her beauty parlor screaming. She's got a darned good case for damages, both for business lost and mental anguish. I tell you . . . . Chuck, are you laughing? Answer me. . . . Answer me. . . ."

Chuck held his hand over the phone mouthpiece. He tried to continue the conversation, but he couldn't restrain his laughter. Finally, he handed the phone to Merl. "Tell him it's the paper's fault," Chuck said, holding his sides from the pain of laughter, "a misprint of the street. Get a man over to accept the rats. The newspapers will print it right tomorrow." Chuck couldn't say any more; the image of Olivia's Beauty Salon overrun with seedy characters toting dead rats was too much. He went out on the front porch, sat on the steps and, in sobs, got control of himself.

45

"What's so funny?" Peter Balantine, the cabdriver, said when he walked up. Balantine was dressed in a sports jacket and tie today, and Chuck thought he looked more like a lawyer than a hack driver. Chuck told Balantine about the mistaken rat delivery. Balantine only smiled politely.

"If you're going to make it as a slumlord," Chuck said, "you'll have to find yourself a sense of humor. Without one you're dead down here."

"Sorry, Mr. Costa. I haven't felt much like joking recently. I got another pile of violations in the mail this morning. My building is being torn apart, and I don't know how to stop it."

Chuck looked at the city violation notices Balantine had. There were at least a dozen for unsafe or unsanitary housing, some for sinks missing, toilets stopped up, walls damaged, and windowpanes broken. "That certainly qualifies you as a slumlord," Chuck said. "Any of this your neglect?"

"No. Not any."

"Hey," Chuck said, "I've got some buildings to check on. Why don't you ride along and tell me about it. I listen better when I'm moving, anyway."

Chuck had barely gotten the car out of the garage and into forward gear when Peter Balantine started telling his story. He had bought the apartment building last year. The place needed lots of small repairs, and Balantine had them all done or did them himself. That meant increased cost, so he raised the rents on the tenants, who were mostly retirees. They moved out, one at a time, and Peter replaced them with younger tenants, marginal-poverty types, yet not on welfare. That's when the damage began: sinks ripped from walls, windows and doors smashed, drains clogged intentionally. The building inspectors suddenly appeared, issuing violations. Shortly thereafter the tenants refused to pay rent until the repairs were made; but without the rent, Balantine said he didn't have the money to make the repairs. Peter made demands on the tenants, but nothing changed. "I tell you," Peter said, "if I can't get some money to fix the place up soon, I'm going to lose it."

Chuck drove and listened. It was an old story by now. Tenants had gotten wise to the fact that as long as violations were pending with the

46

city, they could withhold rents, and the landlord couldn't evict them, so they would rip out a fixture, kick in some walls, then call out the city inspectors, and go on a rent strike. The building, and the landlord, would go under.

"You made about every mistake in the book," Chuck said when Peter lapsed into silence. "Old people are the best tenants you can have. Sure, you can't charge them much rent, but they'll pay promptly and take personal care of the building. Then to let in the new element without any screening—Christ, Peter, you were taking big risks."

"But *you* let in anyone in your buildings. Everybody says so."

"That's not quite true. I cull the crop of troublemakers, the real mean cases. I let everyone else in, but I can handle them. That reminds me. You look like an old friend named Balantine. Are you any relation to Jack Balantine?"

"He was my father," Peter said.

"Why didn't you say so last night? Jack was a fine man, and I owed him a few favors." Chuck remembered Jack Balantine. He was a police sergeant, who had been shot through the head during the riot. "You know your dad drove me around during the riots to collect rents. He didn't want to see my buildings fall down because of that insanity. I was with him the day before he was killed. Why didn't you say Jack was your dad?"

"I don't want favors," Peter said. He looked out the window away from Chuck. "I'm willing to pay for your services as soon as I can."

"Believe me, I won't be doing you any favors by setting you up in this business. You don't know what it takes down here. When I look for building managers, I print the address in the ad. The ones who call say, 'I'm six-two,' 'I carry a baseball bat,' or, 'I'm meaner than hell.' They know that's what it takes to run one of these buildings. No college degrees. Not even reading and writing. Just enough to make out a receipt and back off a hard-assed tenant. That's not enough sometimes. Some of my best men have been robbed blind, mugged and run off."

"I met one of your managers who didn't fit that mold," Peter said. "A small man . . . Jimmy Caldwell. Doesn't he work for you?"

"You've met Jimmy? Well, don't let his baggy pants and slow mouth put you off. Jimmy isn't afraid of anything. That guy's been in and out of

47

jails most of his life. He's mean when someone leans on him, so I stick him in the building with all the drunks and misfits.''

"You keep a building for drunks?''

Chuck turned the corner onto the service drive of the John C. Lodge Expressway. "Sure. I segregate my tenants—old-timers in one, working couples in another, welfare women with kids in another. You name it, I probably have a building full of it. And it works that way. The old don't like kids around. Working people don't get on with welfare types. Nothing strange about that. You wouldn't house a cat and a canary in the same cage, would you?''

Peter hadn't gotten an answer out when Chuck slammed on the brakes and swerved the graceless Cadillac over to the curb. "Look at that,'' Chuck said. He pointed at a hand-lettered "Furniture for Sale'' sign tacked to a screened-in front porch. The sign was obviously made from a cardboard box; the fold in the cardboard ran through the "t'' in "Furniture'' and the "a'' in "Sale.'' The house itself was an ordinary Detroit home, built in the 20s when ornate scrollwork adorned every eave, and every porch had a hanging swing. The house was twenty feet wide and looked twice as tall, like a book standing on end. Yet there were no houses on either side, giving the building an unsupported appearance. Chuck got out and walked to the porch. The screen door was unlocked. It might as well be, Chuck thought, glancing through the triangular rips on every screen frame. Peter followed.

A man, with dimensions similar to the house, answered Chuck's knock. He was tall, yet had a protruding stomach that looked grafted onto his bony frame.

"I'm here about your furniture,'' Chuck said. "How much are you asking?''

The man looked at Chuck for some time, over at Peter's necktie, and back at Chuck again. "Four hundred dollar for everything in the house,'' he said in broken English that Chuck recognized as Spanish.

"*Ay, hablas español,*'' Chuck said. An opening. Chuck continued the conversation in Spanish, raising his voice into the romantic rhythm of the language. Chuck spoke of Mexican people in the neighborhood and passed the word on to the old man that Father Gomez, a local Catholic priest, had planned to return to San Pablo. Was the old man returning to Mexico also?

*"Sí,"* the old man said. *"Ya bastante con America."* He said that he had worked at the Chrysler Plant on Mound Road many years and had planned to return to Mexico in a couple of years. But the city condemned his house, so he would return earlier. He wanted to sell all the furniture, the man said, for four hundred dollars.

"You know," Chuck said, "that when the city condemns a building, they pay an allotment to move you to another house."

*"Es inútil*, I'm leaving the country. They will not pay me for that."

Chuck hesitated for a minute. "Look. If I get you five hundred dollars and have the furniture out today, would you be satisfied?"

"But, of course."

Chuck shook on the deal and was back in the car in a minute. Peter sat alongside with a quizzical wrinkle to his brow.

"I don't get it, Chuck. You're willing to spend a hundred dollars more than the man was asking, and for a houseload of old furniture?"

"I need furniture for a few rooms in my new place on John R. Street. But I'm not going to spend a cent for it. Fact is, I'm going to earn an extra hundred plus the furniture, and I'll even have it moved at the city's expense."

"I don't get it."

"Let it be Lesson One to becoming a slumlord. There's little money to be made down here unless you work the angles. The city, I happen to know, has a regulation on moving expenses on condemned homes. They'll give that man a check for six hundred dollars for incidentals and cover the cost of a mover. All I've got to do is call the city on his behalf, fill out some papers, move him to my John R. building, and—presto, I get the furniture delivered, and I pick up a hundred bucks from our new friend."

"You're a hustler."

The word struck a sensitive nerve, and Chuck could feel his cheeks flushing. "No, I'm a businessman. That man gets more than he wanted. He's happy. I get what I want. And the city gets to shove an old man out of his home—urban renewal, they call it—tear down a solid house to pour some cement for people that are so much in a hurry to get out of town every night that they need an expressway. Maybe paying him a pittance will ease the city's conscience, make a bureaucrat feel noble. So

49

I might be making them happy besides. That's a good deal. Three smiles.''

"I'm not so sure, Costa. It seems to me you're taking advantage of the city.''

"All right. I've got a moralist on my hands. I'll put the old man up in my John R. building before he leaves town. A week's free rent. That way, he's actually moving in. That ought to plug the technicalities,'' Chuck said. He was reminded of Peter's father. He, too, saw everything as right or wrong, black or white. Chuck had liked the father for that incorruptibility, that schoolboy naïveté, and he now found himself liking the son for the same reason. "Tell you what,'' Chuck said. "You stick with me for a couple of weeks, work as my assistant. You'll learn the business, and I'll get some help, not to mention a moral education.''

"In two weeks my tenants will have torn my building down. I won't have any need to learn how to manage.''

"I'll straighten out your mess tomorrow.''

"Just like that,'' Peter said with a burlesque sweep of the hand that told Chuck he didn't believe it was possible. "I've got a dozen safety violations, and tenants on a rent strike, and no money to make repairs, and just like that, just like that, you can make everything right.''

"Why not?''

"Costa,'' Peter said as he tossed up his hands, "you can't be for real.''

"Maybe I'm not. Maybe they'll be laying for us at your building and we'll end up tarred and feathered. Maybe they'll have already leveled the place by the time we get to it. How do I know? Christ, I don't have a crystal ball. But I do know that if you reach out at a dog assuming he's going to bite, you're as good as bitten. You've got to believe we can turn it around, or we can't.''

"Positive thinking isn't going to save my apartments,'' Peter said.

"Nothing else will. I've got it. Let's go over to my new building. That place was a shooting gallery two days ago. Now it's on the way back. You look it over, and I bet you'll catch on to what I'm saying.''


Twenty minutes later Chuck was entering the lobby of his John R. building with his new assistant following a pace behind. Georgie's truck was out front. Chuck knew Georgie would be rushing around directing the cleanup people and repairing the radiators ripped out the night before. Chuck liked the activity, the smell of fresh paint and ammonia. He warmed to the mumble of people talking in the building. And the music, the beat, was coming out over transoms at full volume, not at the half-audible level it had been just yesterday when the dope addicts were on the fourth floor playing king of the castle. The place was coming around to the sweet anarchy of a healthy building. Chuck felt good. It was elation, the kind he speculated a doctor feels when he removes a cancer, or a priest when he baptizes a heathen, a celebration of life that Chuck could feel a part of with each building saved from self-destruction. Such moments as this were the real rent, the payoff for a city landlord. Peter would someday understand. If only his Anita and Ralph understood.

Chuck found Georgie on the second-floor landing replacing a broken windowpane. Chuck introduced Peter. Georgie wiped putty from his hand onto his coverall front, then extended it to Peter.

"Got someone to replace Georgie, 'ey?" Georgie said.

Chuck patted Georgie on the side and looked up at them both. "No, I've decided to start a pro basketball team. You two are my first drafts. Say, Georgie, wasn't that Nancy Maier I saw going into one of the apartments downstairs?"

"Uh-huh. She came over this morning looking for a place. I put her in 1B."

Chuck realized that Peter was left out. "Nancy Maier is a professional baby factory. She's bright enough to know that every time she drops a baby the welfare ups her payments, so she's found her niche."

"She's never been married," Georgie said. "And she's got four kids and pregnant with another. I wonder who knocked her up this time."

"That," Chuck said, "is like getting hit in the ass with a saber saw and wantin' to know which tooth cut you."

"You certainly have a way with words," Peter said. All three men laughed.

Just then a boy burst down the stairs. He pushed behind Peter, forcing him forward on the cramped landing. Chuck recognized the boy immediately. "Martin Luther," he said, "what's your hurry?" The boy

51

stopped, looked up at the three men, then noticeably began to shrink, hunching his shoulders and lowering his head to appear smaller. "Gentlemen, this is Martin Luther. He has a brand-new bandage on his neck." Chuck bent down to Martin's eye level. "Did you get that bandage at the health clinic, Martin?" The boy nodded in a way that kept his head below eye-contact level. "I'll bet they gave you a shot, too. And I'll bet you didn't even cry, not even a little tear. You're brave, that's for sure." Chuck rubbed Martin Luther's wiry head, and as soon as he took his hand back, the boy was gone down the stairs and out the door.

"That kid has a hunk out of his neck where a rat bit him," Chuck said to Peter. "It's enough to make you sick."

"Is he the reason for the rat bounty?" Peter asked.

"Him and a lot like him. But don't get the idea I'm a do-gooder. That rat bounty won't hurt my business any. People will see that Chuck Costa is down here trying to do a job on this town. It's good press, and it brings in more business. Besides, I don't like rats."

"Hey, Chuck," someone called from the lobby, "telephone."

Chuck felt a knot in his stomach. The call would be from Marilyn, and if she had to call him during the rounds, it had to be trouble. He went to the pay phone in the lobby and picked up the dangling receiver. "What is it now?"

"There are two black men here talking rough," Marilyn said. "They say you've got their tools, that the police gave them your address. One named Raymond says you had them arrested. I think they intend to start something."

Chuck remembered that one of the two men he had caught stealing plumbing the night before was named Raymond. "Are any of my managers around?"

"No," Marilyn said. "I think Anita and the kids are in the house, but no one's in the office but those two."

"Stay in my inner office. Get your can of Mace out and hold on," Chuck said. "I'm on my way."

Chuck hung up the receiver and in the same movement was out the door. He heard Peter follow and yell. Chuck didn't stop. He was pulling away from the curb when Peter opened the door and jumped in. The door swung free and scraped along the curb as the Cadillac spun into traffic.

52

In less than five minutes Chuck was on his front porch. He stopped at the door, listened, and took in a long breath. Peter was behind him. Chuck gave a passing thought to the confusion Peter must have been going through, but dismissed it and went inside. Both men sat in the outer office. One was about fifty, with salt-and-pepper gray throughout his close-cropped do. The other man Chuck recognized as Raymond, the man he hadn't shot the night before. Raymond was on the chair about the same way an ironing board would be propped—flattened out and touching in two spots, his neck and his hips. Raymond's long legs stretched well into the middle of the room. He fumbled unconsciously with an ivory elephant that had been on Marilyn's desk. I should have shot him when I had the chance, Chuck thought. I muffed it.

Raymond and his friend came to their feet. Raymond was grinning. "Hey, man. You remember me? I'm da guy you pointed a gun at this mornin'."

"What are you doing here?"

"Loose, man. I just come for my tools. This here is my uncle. They're his tools. I left them in your place."

"Out on bail already?" Chuck asked. He knew it was a rhetorical question.

"Sure." Raymond quivered when he talked, like a six-foot stack of Jell-O. "My buddy, he would of got out, but on account of you messed his leg up, he's still in the hospital. That wasn't right just for some pipes."

The older black man held a cold gaze on Chuck. "You think you a bad mother."

Chuck sized up the old man. His hands were out of his pockets. No knife. Chuck stepped forward to face off with him. Raymond stepped between them.

"Hang loose," Raymond said. "Alls I want is them tools. My uncle here's got to make a living. You got his tools."

"Get your asses out of here before you get something you don't want," Chuck said. He could feel the blood flushing to his face, but he held back. "Next time you see those tools, you'll be in court. And if you come around here before then, you might eat them."

"Bad mother," the old man said as he went for Chuck. Peter

appeared behind the man, put a hand on his shoulder, pressing one finger into the base of his neck. The old man went limp.

"Take it easy," Peter said. "Mr. Costa doesn't want any trouble."

"Oh, yes I do," Chuck said. "Raymond, I'm not dropping any charges, and you're going to jail. Uncle can steal some more tools."

"For some old pipes, man?" Raymond said. His voice rose into a falsetto, and the quivers became pronounced. "You're going to do all that for some goddamned old radiator pipes?"

"Raymond, I'd send you to jail over two cent's worth of copper if I could. Now get out."

The two men left. Raymond sauntered out, and the older man walked bent forward, rubbing the nape of his neck.

Chuck watched them go. "You know," Chuck said, "I honestly believe they thought they had a right to those burglary tools. That's the real crime. Ignorance. Those morons don't know or care that they destroy a fifty-thousand-dollar building for the hundred bucks a junkyard will give for copper pipes. Once the pipes are gone, there's no profit in fixing one of those buildings. How dumb."

"I think they wanted to intimidate you out of testifying against nephew Raymond," Peter said.

"Normally I would have dropped the charges, anyway," Chuck said. "You look surprised. I've taken dozens of these cheap hoods to court. They get off light or scot-free every time. Either the prosecutor plea-bargains them off with a fine, or they plead guilty, and the judge thanks them for admitting they've been bad, slaps their wrists, and sends them off again. In the end, I waste my time sitting in court."

"My dad used to complain about lenient courts, but that didn't stop him from making arrests. If you don't prosecute, there's no chance of justice."

"Your dad got paid for going through the motions. My lost time costs me money. But don't worry, this time I'll push it. I had to shoot one of those guys last night, and if I drop the charges, he could sue me. He might anyway, you know. Free legal clinics love those cases. It doesn't cost them anything to sue. That's justice for you." Chuck turned and headed for his inner office. "By the way," he said, "where did you learn that Kung Fu one-finger stuff you used on that guy?"

"Dad taught me."

"You might have the makings of a slumlord after all. Now all you need is some know-how."

They entered the inner office. Marilyn and Anita both stood behind the desk. Marilyn had an aerosol can of Mace in her hand; Anita had a paring knife in her hand, only partially concealed behind her apron. Both women looked scared.

"Well, look at this," Chuck said. "We didn't have to rush back. There's a whole army that could have taken care of those thugs."

"That's not funny," Anita said, but she smiled as she came around the desk and kissed Chuck on the cheek.

"OK, but they're gone and won't be back. This is Peter Balantine. He's the one who ran them off. Why don't you make him some tea, Anita?"

Chuck went behind the desk and began ruffling through the telephone messages. Marilyn stood alongside, replacing the cap on her Mace canister.

"Did you see this?" Marilyn said. She pushed a newspaper from the edge of the desk to the center. It was a copy of *The Fifth Estate*, the Wayne State University's semi-underground newspaper. Below the decorative masthead was a single boldfaced headline: SLUMLORD BRIBES MISTREATED TENANT. Chuck sat down and read the article. "Slumlord Charles Costa, when confronted by Wayne student activists about unjust eviction of an aged tenant, offered to bribe the complaining black woman with posh accommodations . . . ." The article went on, but Chuck didn't. He recognized the by-line, Susan Stanicki, the blond who had led the protest march.

Chuck grabbed the phone and called his lawyer. "Hello, Ralph. That Fuller woman eviction I canceled? It's on again. You get her out right away, and make sure those college kids hear about it. I don't care what I said before, you just—"

The scream came from the backyard. It was Anita's voice. Chuck dropped the phone and ran. He jumped the four steps down into the backyard. Anita was coming toward the house. She carried little Pepe. His front was covered with blood, his face white. Chuck felt his legs buckling, and a chill ran up his spine. Then he saw what was wrong.

55

Four fingers on Pepe's right hand were gashed open above the knuckles. The raw flesh was exposed. The blood poured out of each gash. Pepe stared at the wound as if it belonged to someone else. Chuck took out his handkerchief and covered the hand so that Pepe couldn't see it. Pepe began to cry. Chuck nudged Anita before him into the car, and they were on their way to the hospital.

"Squeeze his wrist like a tourniquet," Chuck said. He reached across the seat with his right hand and squeezed the boy's wrist to demonstrate. "How did it happen?"

Anita held Pepe close to her breast, rocking gently from side to side in a motion counter to the car's. She took a long time before she answered Chuck. "They're animals, all of them. Pepe was hanging on the storm fence watching the kids come home from school. He always stands there by the fence, waiting for his brothers and sisters. This little kid, a kindergartner, just a little kid, he came up to the fence, grabbed Pepe's hand, and bit him. Like an animal, he just bit Pepe like a dog."

The emergency room was empty. Rush hour at the hospital was after ten P.M. and on weekends, when the fight cases, drug overdoses, and heart attacks came in; but on a weekday afternoon, there was an entire staff to attend a whimpering child. Two nurses and a tall black doctor worked on Pepe's hand. Anita stroked the hair back of Pepe's forehead and whispered reassurances. Chuck stood a few feet away; he felt useless. His son was being sewn up, jabbed with a tetanus needle, and tampered with, and there was nothing he could do but stand by feeling nauseated by the antiseptic smell and the sight of his son's blood.

After the stitching, Anita and Chuck stood at the counter as a corpulent redheaded nurse filled out the report forms.

"Doctor doesn't think he'll lose the use of those fingers," she said. She didn't look up from her writing. "They'll be stiff for a month or two. Sign the release on this line, Mr. Costa. Is 26540 Lincoln a permanent address?"

"I'm not sure," Chuck said. "We may be moving out to the suburbs soon, real soon." Anita looked up at Chuck and leaned her weight against his arm. Nothing more needed saying.

# 4

Peter Balantine stood at the top of the stairs clad in powder-blue pajamas and terry cloth robe. It was eight A.M. by his watch, and he was impatient to get going. "Hey, Mom," he yelled, "where's my blue sports coat?"

His mother appeared in the kitchen door with a sizzling skillet still in hand. "It's at the cleaners. Why don't you wear the brown suit? I polished your brown shoes just yesterday."

"Sure," he said, and went back to his room thinking to himself how the blue jacket would have been better. The blue jacket was his favorite, he felt best in it, and Peter suspected it was lucky. He got out the brown suit and picked out a yellow shirt and yellow-brown patterned tie. All were laid on the bed in the order he would put them on—shirt, suit, then tie. As was his custom, he then went into the bathroom to shave.

Peter pressed the electric razor firm against his jaw and felt the frantic lilliputian blades snip at his chin hairs. Shaving was a morning exercise to Peter, like his twelve push-ups and twenty deep knee-bends, for Peter's facial hair was so blond that if his razor missed a spot, it still wouldn't be visible the next morning. This morning shaving received no thought at all as he mulled ahead through the day. He was to meet Costa again today. For what, Peter wasn't sure. Another lesson on landlording, perhaps. Peter had been under Costa's tutelage for three weeks now. He had learned much, but not the important answer of how to save his apartment building. Maybe this would be the day Costa would invade his building and place him back in authority. He wanted that, now more than ever, yet the thought of walking back in, of facing the tenants, petrified him. He had endured many abuses at the hands of his tenants—garbage smeared over his cár, insults, and outright defiance of his position. But the last encounter had been in front of Sheila. The knives, the jeers, the boy spitting on his trousers, and Sheila standing by with a benign look that he had felt pierce him, the look Peter had taken for pity. Why did she matter? He wasn't really certain. Sheila Meade was a tenant, Apartment 27. She was one of the few who paid her rent, yet she had also paid Peter in friendship. She would talk to him while he was making repairs, this ragtag waif with soft, brown eyes. She listened and she consoled. Perhaps he would see Sheila today. The thought frightened and stirred him. He set the razor aside, meticulously combed his hair, sprayed it, dressed, then went downstairs.

The house was shrouded in gray half-light. The sun was well up outside, but the jack pines and oak trees that stood sentinel around the entire house allowed past only a select number of rays. On the wall at the foot of the stairs was a wooden plaque, shaped like a police badge. On it was a patch of black velvet, also badge-shaped, and centered on the cloth was badge number 1174. The men in his father's precinct had presented the plaque to his mother just after the funeral, and now it hung where it did to draw notice by anyone using the stairs in the small bungalow, which was everyone, since the only bathroom was upstairs. Peter wished he could put it away.

The kitchen smelled of bacon grease as Peter entered. The dinette table was ready for him. His mother came to the table and poured coffee. Peter took his place, unfolded the *Royal Oak Tribune,* and lifted his cup. The process had been ritual for as many of Peter's twenty-four years as he could remember; only before his father's murder, Peter had sat on his mother's side of the table and waited for his father to pass each newspaper section across to him when he was finished. Peter, in turn, would pass each section to his mother when finished. It was the pecking order, and though shortened, it remained intact.

58

"Are you going down to see your Mr. Costa again?" his mother said.

"He's not *my* Mr. Costa, Mom. I told you, he's a big landlord who's going to help me with the apartment building."

"You could have gone to your uncle Bert for help," she said. She was looking down at her plate, jabbing her fork at the eggs. Peter watched her scalp where the gray roots of her brown hair showed. "Those people would pay if your Uncle Bert came calling in his uniform."

"Mom, they aren't about to pay a pig, not even a sergeant pig."

"Pig?" Her eyes rushed up at Peter. "Your father wasn't a pig. Neither is your uncle. They're . . . ."

"Law enforcement officers," Peter answered. "But even the police call themselves pigs now. It's like 'cop.' No disrespect at all. Bert even has a sweat shirt with 'pig' on the chest."

"Well, they're not pigs, they're police officers. Those people listen to policemen. Uncle Bert would come down there with you. I asked him."

Peter put his cup down. "Nobody told you to ask him. I can handle this without you or Bert."

"Don't talk to me like that," she said. She sat up perfectly straight. Peter knew she was angry. "If your father were alive, you wouldn't talk to me like that. He wouldn't let you shout at your mother."

"That's hitting below the belt. Besides, I wasn't shouting," Peter said. He realized as he said it that that, too, came out in a shout. "All I said was I didn't need any help."

"Then why did you go to this Costa? Is that an I-talian name? Dear God, you're not mixed up with the Mafia?"

"Come off it, Mom. Chuck Costa is Maltese. He's not even Italian. I don't think he's connected to anything." Peter got up from the table and headed for the coat closet in the front room.

"You don't know for sure, do you?" she said, tagging behind him. "Uncle Bert can check the blotter. He'd find out if that man's I-talian."

Peter turned around and looked down at her as he put on his overcoat. "Leave Bert out of this, please. I'm not going to get involved in anything I can't get out of. Can't you this once trust me?" He paused, then shook his head in self-disgust. "I know your money's in the building, too, but it's going to work out. I'm doing the right thing. Costa's one of Dad's friends. He's going to help me settle the rent strike." Peter leaned down and kissed her on the forehead before she could rebut him, then he backed out of the front door.

"You going to drive the cab tonight?" she said.

"Yes, Mom." He was halfway down the front steps.

"I can make you some sandwiches."

"No thanks, I'll grab a burger."

"You can't drive the cab in your suit. It'll get all wrinkled."


Peter shifted repeatedly as he piloted his Volkswagen through the traffic on Woodward Avenue. He thought about his mother between maneuvers. He hadn't told her how serious the situation was. There was a rent strike, he had said, that's all. Any more of a disclosure and she would have had the entire seven-thousand-man police force swinging night sticks. She had lived for thirty years in the tight-knit circle of police wives, and Peter believed she thought they were invincible, even now, even after Dad was shot to death on the job. Dad hadn't been able to talk to her either. Argue together, pray together, but not confide, talk. Several times in the last couple of days Peter had wanted to tell his mother about Costa. Peter had his doubts about this crazy man who assumed he could straighten out the building, just like that, as if it were a disputed basket at a church social. He wanted to tell his mother how flippant, how cocksure the man was, yet he somehow knew that if anyone could save the building, Costa could. Sheila would understand, even if Mother couldn't, Peter thought, and his fantasies about the tenant girl began anew.

Twenty minutes later Peter was still driving on Woodward, but it wasn't the same thoroughfare he had turned onto in Royal Oak. The eight-lane highway with a green median had become a crowded city street, the main street of Detroit. The green lawns and parks had given way, block by block along his route, to cement, and yellow litter boxes. Palatial restaurants in Royal Oak were six-stool diners here. Camera shops, pet emporiums, and unisex boutiques in Royal Oak were reduced

60

to pawn shops, bars, and celluloid burlesque houses here. Signs, posters, arcades all blurred together to assault and bewilder the senses. Yet, as if to remind Peter that this was still Woodward Avenue, a grand cathedral or a stately building was juxtaposed against the squalor. That was what Detroit was all about to Peter—contrast that confused him. Fetid vomit on the street where perfume lingered from a debutante ball, contrast that could praise the heroism of his father against the cries of protesters picketing for the man who had shot him. Peter wanted no part of the contrast, no part of becoming a dead hero. He didn't care what the family thought of him for not becoming a cop. Why should he die for people who didn't care? He had everything to live for. The city wasn't going to kill him. Peter had bought the building here only because he couldn't afford to start in business in the posh suburban apartment world. He'd make a profit here, he had planned, then invest in a garden apartment building in Royal Oak, or maybe Birmingham. The plan had been dashed by the vandalism and the tenant strike, but now there was Costa, the crusty foreigner with fire enough in him to rekindle Peter's ambitions.

Peter turned off Woodward onto Seldon Street. He automatically reached across and locked the passenger-side door, then let up on the accelerator. Costa had asked Peter to meet him at one of his buildings, 1603 Seldon St. There it was. Nice. A three-story brick. The paint over the brick was recent, Peter concluded from the paint drips edging every window. The brick was navy gray, the trim black. Several windowpanes had no paint drippings and were so clear that Peter decided they, too, must be new. Costa's going to show off some recent rehabilitation, he concluded.

Inside, the halls were as clean as the outside, with the same gray paint theme prevailing, yet with white ceilings. Peter was hunting for the manager's apartment when he saw Costa down the hall talking to a sandy-haired man in overalls. Costa was wearing a bright blue-green sports jacket and the turtleneck sweater that Peter concluded must be his trademark. Every time Peter saw Costa he was surprised how small the man was. Costa couldn't have been more than five feet eight or nine, muscular, but not stocky by any measure. Why was it, Peter thought, after a few minutes with Costa he always saw him as imposingly large,

61

and every time he saw Costa after an interlude of several hours he shrank again?

Costa must have noticed Peter coming. He waved him on without breaking his conversation with the man in overalls. As Peter came within hearing range, he picked out a few plumbing terms and concluded that the man was here to do some repairs.

"Thirty-five ought to do it pretty much," Costa said. Peter thought he detected a Southern accent in Costa's speech. "Oh, this here boy is Pete Balantine. Pete's working for me for a while. Pete, this is Bill Skinner, best damn hillbilly handyman going."

"How do you do?" Pete said. He tried to look the handyman in the eyes instead of staring at the tangle of hair protruding from each nostril. "Do you manage this building?"

"No, sir," Skinner said. Peter thought that must have struck him funny because the man smiled, revealing the first grader's malady of missing front teeth. "I don't but work a couple of hours now and again."

"He won't work," Costa said. "I've pestered him to manage a building, even this one. It doesn't have a manager. But no, Bill doesn't want to lose his welfare checks. Tell Pete why you ain't workin', Bill. Go on, tell him why you won't work."

Bill Skinner looked Pete over, and he felt as if he were being stripped, weighed, then stamped on the shank with a Grade-A approval. "Count 'a I ain't paying no taxes to support no niggers on welfare."

Chuck laughed, though he had obviously heard the line before. "But it's all right that *I* pay taxes to support hillbillies, right?"

"You know that ain't so," Skinner said. "I'd take a job right off, 'cept I can't afford it."

"I'm afraid I don't understand," Peter said.

"He right enough?" Skinner said, looking to Costa. Costa nodded, and Skinner pointed his carpeted nose back at Peter. "Well, Charlie here will give me 'bout four hundred a month to run this place. Welfare gives me near three hundred not to do it. I can make up the other hundred with odd jobs in a week's time, more or less. The other three weeks is gravy."

"You see, Pete," Costa said, "the government is my competitor. I can't pay men the kind of money to keep them off welfare. But you can't blame Bill. He came north to make some money, and he's doing just that."

Peter couldn't believe what Costa was saying. The man was cheating on welfare, and Costa was siding with him. Peter tried not to let his face show his quandary.

"Yes, sir," Skinner said. "Soon as I get some tucked away, I'm going back home. This town is stinkin' with niggers. Then I ain't comin' back. Goddamn it, I'll shoot my best bird dog dead just for pointin' north."

Costa took a roll of bills from his front pocket, peeled off thirty-five dollars, and gave it to Skinner. After some final words Skinner left and Costa led Peter into the manager's apartment. Once in the door, Peter couldn't hold himself back any longer.

"Why are you encouraging a welfare cheat?"

"I'm not. You heard me offer him a job."

"But you're paying him for jobs in cash?" Peter was irritated, and he no longer cared to hide it.

"I'm glad you arrived in time to meet Bill," Costa said. "He's one of the reasons I wanted you to come before we tackle your place. Now you tell me what to do. Say you can't find a plumber who'll work cheap enough to keep up these low-income units. Do you let the pipes leak? Let tenants go without? No way. You pay anyone who'll do the work. Bill would manage this place, too, if I'd pay him on the q.t. I won't go that far, but when I can't get a small job done, I'm not above bringing Bill in."

Peter wanted to say more, but he clenched his teeth. He needed Costa today. If the man was an opportunist, Peter reasoned, that was his problem. Let it alone this time. "OK," Peter said, "that's your business."

"No, it's not OK." Costa turned his back on Peter and walked over to the couch. The room was completely furnished in Salvation Army pieces. The lack of anything on tables or mantle said the apartment was vacant. Costa sat on the edge of the couch arm, lit a Chesterfield, then stared back at Peter.

"You wanted me to put you straight. That's what I'm doing. It's not OK. It's goddamn right. . . ."

"That's your—"

"Don't butt in," Costa said. His eyes were narrow, and Peter saw they meant business. "You let me tell you why you're here before you say another word, or, so help me, I'll toss you out and let your tenants finish eating your ass."

Peter held Costa's stare for what seemed like minutes. Neither man spoke. Finally Peter turned away and went over to the room's lone chair. He dropped into it. "OK," Peter said, "I'm here to learn."

"That's more like it." The lines of Costa's face unfolded, and he slipped down onto the couch cushion. "I want you to meet some of my people in this building."

Peter looked at his watch.

"Don't sweat it," Costa said. "We've got enough time. You see, this is my experimental building. It's working for me even though I don't have a manager just now. The last owner gave it to me, scot-free. The tenants were withholding rent and the whole bit. Now it pays."

"You got rid of the troublemakers," Peter said.

"Uh-uh, it's the same bunch I inherited. Fifty-five families. All on public doles. All but five or six without any men in the place." Chuck got up and started for the door. Peter's curiosity was aroused, and he quickly followed.

"Then how did you get them to pay?"

"I didn't. *They* did. I helped them work up a tenants' union. Real rights. They can demand I change things, and I got to do it under the agreement. They could even evict a bad manager. In fact, that's why there's no manager now." Costa went up the stairs. He continued to talk to Peter in a louder voice to overcome the music coming out of the rooms. "Tenants have the right to fine their own members. If someone screws up the place for the others, she has to pay a buck or two fine. If she bitches, she can move out."

"You mean you abdicated control?"

"Abdicated, humm. I guess you could say that. Actually, I gave them some say in their own homes. And they've been tougher on offenders than Chuck Costa could be. You see, there's only a few bad

64

ones in any building, so I figured if the others had their say . . . . Well, it's worked so far."

They were on the third floor now, and Costa went up to one of the doors and knocked. "Each level has a floor captain, gets ten bucks off the rent. This is one of them."

"Yeh?" a high-pitched voice came from behind the door. "Who's it?"

"Chuck Costa. You going to make me stand out here all day?"

The door opened wide, and a redheaded woman stood in it. Peter was surprised. She was a shapely woman, if the outline in the thin shortie nightgown held true. Her hair was frizzled, and her eyelids were laden with misapplied makeup, yet the eyes beneath were a startling pale green. Chuck patted her on the hip and walked in. Peter wasn't sure, but he followed. The room was laden with the suffocating aroma of incense, or perhaps dime store perfume, Peter wasn't certain which. The radio was on full blast. Eddie Arnold was singing a gospel tune, but Peter couldn't make out the words because of the volume. In the kitchen two little girls were playing at the table with some papers. They looked toward Peter, then ran into the living room.

"Mr. Chuck," one of the girls said and grabbed Costa by the leg, "you bring us anything?" The other girl stood by with her hands down.

"Lay off him," the woman said. She took a swipe at the one who had said nothing. Peter figured it was because that girl was closest. "Get your asses in the kitchen and leave us be."

"Hold on, Mildred," Costa said. "They're not bothering us." He reached down and mussed the clinging girl's hair. "I just stopped in to let you meet my new assistant. His name's Pete."

Mildred went over to the radio. The news was coming on, and she didn't seem to like it. The volume was turned all but off. "So," she said, "we got ourselves a boy manager. Nice."

"No. He's no manager. I wouldn't put him in this harem. He wouldn't know what to do with all you girls."

Peter didn't like the comment, but he let it go. Mildred looked at him, and he could have sworn she winked.

"Any hassles on your floor?" Costa asked.

"Shit, no. Since we kicked out Rachel and her goddamned flea

65

circus, you'd think this was Iowa or someplace. That whore sure had a gang of dogs,'' Mildred said. She plopped down into a grand over-stuffed chair with rolled padded arms.

"Six dogs," Costa said.

"More like sixteen," she said. "I think she was lettin' 'em screw her—leastwise, you'd think she was by the racket they put up. You'd howl, too, if you had to screw that old whore.''

Mildred rubbed her hip against the chair as she talked, then she ran one leg up onto the chair arm and draped it over. The long pale length of leg was exposed, and Peter's eye was forced to follow the white road to its ultimate junction. She had no pants on. Peter tried not to look directly. He felt uneasy, and certain she was watching him for a reaction.

Costa leaned toward Mildred; the little girl still clung to his leg. He gripped Mildred's dangling ankle and moved her leg back over the chair arm. "Opening for business a little early today, aren't you?" Costa said.

Mildred took on a look of embarrassment, Peter thought, but he decided that he might be reading his own reaction into her droll expression. She hardly seemed like the blushing type.

"Don't we have to go?" Peter said.

"Yeh. Mildred, you call me if any problems come up, you hear?''

"Chuck, honey, if anything comes up, it ain't no problem I can't handle." Costa and Mildred grinned. Peter smiled, too, but he was sure they could see his face redden.

As they went back down the stairs, Peter was regaining his composure. His ears stopped burning, yet he couldn't help feeling foolish. Why had Costa brought him up to see that prostitute? He wanted to ask, but Costa was three steps ahead of him all the way into the manager's vacant apartment. Costa went directly to the telephone and dialed. "Just be a minute," Costa said without looking. "This is rent day and I've got to see how my collections are going. Hello, Merl. Uh-ha . . . yes.''

Peter went over to the window to check on his car. He looked down on the street. No one was out. His car appeared unscathed by his absence. He had had his VW stripped of hubcaps and broken into twice while he was in his own building, and since then he hated to leave it

66

unchaperoned. It was probably too cold out for car stripping, Peter thought, but he took a second glance up and down the block anyway. Costa put down the phone.

"Why can't those philanthropic clowns leave us alone?" Costa said. The lines on his face were drawn.

"What?"

"That damned new law sending the money directly to tenants. Demeaning to have bills paid for them. Bull. I tell you Peter, that law is going to cost us a lot of rents." Costa lit a Chesterfield and drew in so hard that Peter expected the entire cigarette to be consumed in the one inhalation. "It's like putting the cat to guard the canary. If they were able to handle money, they wouldn't *be* on welfare."

"Are your rents down?" Peter asked.

"Yes, but I'll get the money. I've just got to figure an angle around this thing," Costa said. Peter sensed worry in the man for the first time. It came across Costa's face the way a summer cloud blocks the sun and is gone again before one looks up. "Well, what did you think of Mildred?"

"She's a tramp. I really don't get your reason for showing her off."

"She's one of my best tenants, an ADC mother who supplements her government checks on her back. I've got half a dozen like her in every building, plus my assortment of freaks and queers. I was going to show you Glenny up on the fourth floor, too. He's Glen half the time, Glenna the other half—nylon panty hose and all. Why, I remember once. . . ."

"What's the point?" Peter said. "You think I've never seen whores and homos before? Come on, Chuck, give me some credit."

Costa butted his cigarette out and immediately reached inside his jacket for another. "I guess the point is, they're good tenants. They don't bother others, and they pay their rents. Down here you don't ask who's sleeping with what; you don't care. To be a landlord, you've got to accept people as they are. You accept."

"It seems to me those kinds of people cause trouble."

"Some do, and when they do, you knock heads together, kick some asses, but you don't judge. If they're wrong, you might as well pretend they're right and get the hell out of their way."

67

Peter sat on the window ledge realizing as soon as he did that it was blanketed with dust. He got up and brushed at the back of his trousers. Christ, he thought, I may have to go home and change before work after all.

"This is my best building, and it's a menagerie," Costa said. He shrugged his shoulders. "Why, I've got a guy in the basement who is such a crud he can fall out of bed and not drop an inch because of all the junk piled up around him. And then up on the fourth floor there's Mrs. Clean. That old lady has worn inches of surface off the floors just scrubbing."

"I'd rather rent to the Mrs. Cleans," Peter said, now brushing his palms together to shake off the dust.

"Don't be so sure. Last week Mrs. Clean was cleaning out the bathroom. It bugged her so much that there was some dirt she couldn't get at that she pulled the old tub out to clean behind it. Broke the pipes, naturally. Flooded the apartment below hers before we could get it fixed. That's part of what Skinner is doing here. He's bolting down the tub so she won't do it again."

Costa headed for the door and Peter followed him. Outside the air was icy, mid-forties, Peter thought. It's going to be snowing soon.

"Ya know, this place is working," Costa said. Peter watched him glance back at the building as if it were his mistress. "Because I let it. They're freaks, but they all want a decent place to live. They got involved enough to keep it up. I encouraged them, because I like them."

"Yes, I noticed you liked Mildred quite a lot."

"You know," Costa said, "you've got a way of making that sound dirty. I like them, I don't screw them."

"I didn't mean—"

"Maybe not, but it sure as hell sounded like it. Look, I get maybe a dozen chances a week to screw myself out of the rent with women like Mildred. That only causes trouble in a building. Even a dog knows enough not to piss in his plate. You accept them, you don't move in on them."

Peter understood the words. He had heard his father say, "Familiarity breeds contempt." But he couldn't help thinking of Sheila. If she'd let him close, he thought, he wouldn't care about the others.

68

Costa came to his car and stopped. "Enough preaching. I think you're ready to back down those tenants."

"Are we going to my building now?"

"Tomorrow at ten. That's the soonest I could set up a meeting with the tenants. They'll be laying for us. I even invited the tenant rights guys in for them."

"But they're the ones who stirred everyone up. They encouraged my tenants to go on a rent strike."

"I know. They're madder than hell at you," Costa said. He had a devilish grin on his face as he opened his Cadillac door. "This is where they put your foot to the fire."

"That's not funny," Peter said. The thought entered his mind that Costa was setting up an execution for the entertainment of it all. "Maybe we should have some more people on our side there."

"No muscle, no guns this time," Costa said. "You can't thug your tenants into paying rent."

"Then I'm not really sure what we can do."

"To be totally honest," Costa said as he got in his car, "I'm not sure either. But we'll find out tomorrow."

# 5

The gun was wrapped in newsprint and tied with a dozen blue rubber bands. It was wrapped carefully, so much so that it retained the distinctive shape of an army .45-caliber automatic. Of course the shape didn't mean anything to Martin Luther when he saw the wad of paper wedged between a broken baseboard and radiator pipe, but the rubber bands did. He reached for the rubber bands and discovered the gun.

The find was hardly an accident, for Martin had searched the abandoned building floor by floor, room by room. He wasn't looking for a loaded gun, of course, but for treasures only an eleven-year-old could appreciate. In the other abandoned buildings along John R. he had ferreted out a ceramic cat with one ear missing, a quarter tucked deep in the recess of a three-legged couch, and a stack of comic books in a closet. But a gun. That was serious stuff. Martin wrapped it back up with hands that didn't want to work right. The newspaper tore, and the bands didn't go back on straight, but that was close enough for Martin. He jammed the ragged package back into its recess and stumbled several times in his rush out the back door. Martin ran the block back to his apartment building, his lungs aching from cold air drawn in too fast and too often. He visualized the man who owned the gun coming after him, a big white man with hollow eyes. Martin got in the back door quickly and slammed the door behind him. He looked up, and there was the man. A giant in black leather with mean, honky looks. Martin felt his breathing stop and his limbs stiffen. In a while the Gargantua looked down at Martin and smiled. Martin realized he was safe. This was the deaf man that he'd seen with Mr. Costa. He wasn't the man who had hid the gun. Martin Luther wasn't sure of that, and he wasn't about to stick around and find out. He squeezed past Jo-Jo and ran into his apartment.

"Don't slam that door," Mrs. Brown said, as Martin Luther entered. He headed for his room. "Come back here, you. What's you up to, pantin' like the devil's on your tail?"

"Nothin', Mama," he said, as he consciously tried to stop his gasping for air. "I was playing, s'all."

She was ironing. The board was set up in the living room, and she was standing behind it and looking across at a daytime TV show. Mama seemed to be ironing most of the time, and even when she wasn't, the ironing board was always up and used as a shelf for movie magazines and stuff. Not that the apartment wasn't orderly; his mother always kept it neat as a pin and kept after the boys to put things away.

"Where's your brother?" she said without taking her eyes off the TV or her hand off the iron.

"Playing, I guess."

"Then why ain't you with him?" She threw an irritated stare into him. "How come you can't make friends like Noah do? Don't you like people or something?"

Martin Luther was still trying to hide the last vestiges of heavy breathing. He didn't know how to answer.

"Go on to your room, Martin Luther. You ain't no company, anyhow."

Martin went into his room before his mother could think of a new direction for him. If he waited too long in one spot, she'd get on him to do something, he thought. Martin jumped on his bed. There were two beds in the room, one for his younger brother Noah, and his. They filled the room so that there wasn't more than a two-shoe space between the two. Martin rolled up in a ball and pulled the blankets over from the side to cover him. There were about six thin blankets on his bed, and he used all of them to hide beneath now. Maybe he should have taken the gun, he thought. Then if the owner came after him, he would be able to protect himself. He could give the gun to Mama, but she'd have a fit. She'd told him not to play in those empty buildings, or she'd beat him good. And she wouldn't believe how he'd found it, either. Think I stole it, or something, he thought. No, he'd best get the gun and hide it under the bed. His mama was so big she couldn't get down between the beds in the small room. She tried once, he remembered, and almost got stuck. Since then, Martin knew he had a safe place to hide things. Martin decided he'd keep the gun. If someone bothered his mama, he could shoot them. He thought of his mama's friend, Sam. He'd been coming around a lot lately. Sam had a whiskey breath and silver speckle all over his shirt that he once said was shingle dust from his job as a roofer's assistant. He'd sit at the kitchen table and drink with mama or go with her, giggling, to her bedroom. Martin didn't like Sam, and he thought how Sam might hurt Mama. That didn't seem probable, even to Martin, since Sam was scrawny, and Mama would make three of him. Still, it could happen. Sam could hurt her when he was in the bedroom with her. Martin imagined his mama screaming, and him coming in with his gun. He'd shoot Sam right there on the bed, and his mama would thank him and never think to ask where he had gotten the gun. Martin was putting the finishing touches on shooting Sam in his imagination when he heard a knock at the door. He burrowed deeper into his pile of summer blankets.

Chuck knocked hard on Mrs. Brown's door to intervene on the TV soap opera he could hear blaring through the wall. He knocked a second time, and the noise stopped abruptly; the door opened. There stood Mrs. Brown in all of her obesity. What a cow, Chuck thought, and then said, "Good afternoon, Mrs. Brown. You're looking fit today. Say, have you seen Jo-Jo around? I was to meet him here at one, and—"

"Mr. Costa! Martin Luther, Mr. Costa's here. Put the coffee water on."

"Thanks, but I've got to run. I've got a problem in another building that I need Jo-Jo's help on. Have you seen him?"

"No, I ain't, but I'll send Martin Luther to fetch him up. Martin Luther, come out here!"

Martin came out with this head tilted down. He held back, stopping slightly behind his mother. Chuck looked at the boy, but from where he stood, Mrs. Brown's arm was in his view. The arm drew more attention. It was V-shaped, broad at the biceps and tapered down to a wrist and hand too slight to belong to the massive arm. The arm was bumpy with globs of fat that had nowhere to squeeze into the flesh, and veins that popped out also, bright blue veins, ruptured from the strain of feeding blood to the copious mass. How could little Martin hold his head up, Chuck thought, with that mountain of a woman forever leaning on him?

"Martin Luther," she said, "you go fetch Mr. Costa's friend. You know, the deaf and dumb man. He's 'round here someplace, so you fetch him down here." She grabbed Martin by the nape of the neck, and the boy flinched. Chuck wondered if she had dug into the rat scar on his neck. She pushed Martin past Chuck and out the door. Chuck watched him disappear around the corner and thought he should have gone looking for Jo-Jo himself. The boy might wander off and forget it. Chuck decided he'd make some conversation and give the boy a few minutes to try.

"You know, Mrs. Brown, Georgie tells me you've helped him around here to fix the place up. He says you even went down and fixed that washing machine in the basement all by yourself."

"Yes, sir. My daddy was a handyman down in Birmingham. I didn't have no brothers, so's he put me to doing the helper jobs. I guess I learned some that way."

"I could use a person like you to manage this building. No one will take the job," Chuck said, glancing down the hall for a trace of Jo-Jo or the boy.

"You serious, Mr. Costa? I mean, I could keep the place up if you're serious."

Her words drew his attention. Chuck was so used to being turned down trying to hire a manager that he seldom asked without making a joke of it. And here was Mrs. Brown volunteering. Well, why not? She was handy, firm, and big enough so that no tenant in his right mind would attempt to hassle her.

74

"Sure, I'm serious. Can you write well enough to make out receipts?"

"I graduated from high school, Mr. Costa."

"The job pays four hundred dollars a month plus free rent. Now I know that's not much more than you're getting on ADC, but . . . ."

"That's good money. I don't want to be on welfare if I can help it. I never liked charity, no how."

"That's great!" Chuck said. He saw Jo-Jo coming. "I'll have my secretary—you remember Merl?—I'll have her and one of the men come over tomorrow and show you what needs to be done. If you still want to work then, she'll put you on the payroll."

"I can do it, Mr. Costa. I can."

"Great," Chuck said. He took her hand and shook it warmly, remarking to himself on how her hand was smaller than his own. "We've got a deal. You have any trouble, you call me. Now, I've got to run." Chuck backed away and, motioning to Jo-Jo, headed for the front door.

"You won't be sorry, Mr. Costa," Mrs. Brown called after him. "I'll manage this place fine."

As Chuck drove, he explained to Jo-Jo what he was needed for. Chuck found it difficult to talk in sign language and keep the car on the road, too, but he managed. He explained that Jimmy had had to tell a real mean character to move out. A rent evader. The man got nasty and threatened to sic his dog loose on him. Jimmy didn't like the idea of tangling with the dog's yellow teeth, so he called Chuck.

Jimmy was standing in the lobby when Chuck pulled up. Jimmy was leaning against the glass door, looking more like a vagrant than a building manager with a problem. Chuck and Jo-Jo came in.

"Where is he, Jimmy?"

"Ah, he's up in his apartment. I told him to get out. Shit, he's got this dog up there. It ain't my job to fight off no dog."

"Which apartment?"

"Oh, two-oh-eight. But he's got that dog in with him."

Chuck headed up the stairs with Jo-Jo close behind. As he climbed, Chuck heard crashing sounds. That nut's tearing my apartment up, he thought, and took the rest of the steps two at a time. He got to the door, and, without stopping to knock, kicked it in. The dog lurched out the door, past Chuck, and down the stairs. The man stood in the middle of the room, still, as Chuck and Jo-Jo entered.

"He had to piss," the man said. "He'd of chewed your asses off if he didn't have to piss so bad."

Chuck thought how lucky he was that nature had called, and he would have laughed it off, but the room sobered him. The fixtures were torn from the walls. The plasterboard was kicked in on every wall. The floor was strewn with white plaster, electrical fixtures, and broken chairs. The man stood in the midst of the mess. He was a big man with massive hunched shoulders, yet with an expression, Chuck thought, of a small boy caught in the act. Chuck walked around the room as casually as he could, inspecting the damage; around the room, and around the man who stood staring at Jo-Jo by the door.

"Hi, how are ya?" Chuck said. I have him now, he thought, no hurry. "Are you on my payroll? Am I paying you for all this work? Do I owe you something?"

The man didn't answer. Chuck kept smiling as he positioned himself squarely in front of the man, then struck him in the mouth. Chuck took his sweet time between blows, giving him every opportunity to strike back. He didn't, and after three strikes from Chuck's right hand, the man was on the floor, still looking more at Jo-Jo than at his attacker.

Chuck noticed a cardboard box next to the door. It was filled with clothing. "Going somewhere? Fine. We'll help you pack."

Chuck dumped the cardboard box out onto the floor, then picked up two shirts from the pile, neatly folded them, and placed them in the box. He then scooped up some plaster from the floor, placing it in on top of the shirts. Chuck picked up a light fixture and tossed it in on top. "Now you do the rest," he said. He yanked the man by the collar. "Big shot. You pay no rent, then tear the place up when you're asked to leave. Now you clean it up. Your stuff and all of this mess. All in that box."

Chuck and Jo-Jo stood over him as the man picked up clothes and debris and placed it in the box. Jo-Jo went into the kitchen and came back out with a bowl of leftover spaghetti, a plate of chicken, and a half-gallon carton of milk.

"Well, friend, Jo-Jo thinks you forgot some food. I'll just help you pack it up.'' Chuck took the leftovers and poured them into the box, a little at a time: one layer of clothes, one layer of food, one of plaster, and broken furnishings. The box was finally filled above the brim.

"You pick up your box of goodies and get out. And tell your buddies how Chuck Costa let you leave with more than you brought in.''

Chuck and Jo-Jo followed him down the stairs and to the door, nudging him on whenever he looked as if he were going to drop the overloaded box. They watched him out the door and down the street, and Jo-Jo laughed in the high pitch unique to deaf-mutes.

"What did he do to you?'' a voice said from behind. Chuck turned to see Ralph O'Hara standing just inside Jimmy's apartment.

"He tore my place up,'' Chuck said. He could see that Ralph was upset.

"You could have called the police.''

"For what? They'd only toss him out. I want him to remember my farewell. Next time, he might think about ripping up someone else's property.''

"You can't beat them all up, Chuck. Five thousand tenants, and pretty soon none of the lot will be paying rent.'' Ralph talked and rubbed his vest at the same time, a habit Chuck recognized as one of Ralph's nervous quirks. "That is, if any are still paying. Marilyn tells me the direct welfare payments has cut your receipts in half already.''

"Merl tells me the same thing,'' Chuck said. He tried to bring out a smile but couldn't manage it. Jo-Jo came over and pulled the cigarettes out of Chuck's jacket pocket. He lit two, handing one to Chuck. Chuck nodded a thanks, then looked back at Ralph. "Look, Ralph, don't worry. I've decided to sell off a couple of buildings for some operating dough.''

"And who will you be selling to? Everyone is being hit by those direct payments. If you had sold three weeks ago when I told you—''

"Hold it, Ralph, do you hear that?'' Chuck said. He looked up the stairs.

Ralph looked up the stairs and cocked his head. "All I hear is loud music.''

"No, it sounds like a baby crying.''

"So what's so odd about that? This is an apartment house, of sorts.''

77

"It's the *way* it's crying," Chuck said. "It doesn't sound right."

"You're changing subjects on me again, and I'm not letting you get away with it. I came here to tell you about those students and to remind you we've got court tomorrow."

Chuck started up the stairs toward the crying. Ralph followed and kept talking.

"Did you hear me? Those students are after you again, pickets and all. They've been making threatening calls to my office."

"Mine, too," Chuck answered, still climbing toward the sound.

"Well, they mean business. The police told me that leader of theirs, that Susan Stanicki, is linked up with the SDA. That's a revolutionary bunch. Violent."

Chuck walked down the hall on the third floor, homing in on the door where the cries were coming from. "Those students are just kids," he said.

"All the more reason to fear them."

Chuck stopped and looked at Ralph as if he were crazy. "I've got too many other things going just now to worry about school kids starting revolutions. You handle it."

"OK, I'll put Matty Fuller back in an apartment."

"Like hell, you will," Chuck said. "Matty's out. Now do me a favor and go get Jimmy downstairs. Tell him to get up here quick."

Jimmy arrived minutes later with Ralph and Jo-Jo following. Chuck kept listening at the door. "Whose apartment, Jimmy?"

"Shit, Chuck. I don't remember all their names. It's just some hooker. She's got a couple of kids."

Chuck knocked hard on the door. No one answered. He waited and knocked again. Still nothing. But the cries could still be heard—low and long.

"When's the last time you seen her?" Chuck said. He didn't know why, but he was certain something was terribly wrong.

"I don't know. A week. I don't watch 'em."

Chuck took the ring of keys from Jimmy's belt and unlocked the door. He began pushing it open, but there was something in the way. He looked down to see a small head. He fell to his knees and reached inside to push the little body far enough away to enter. The child rolled over enough for him to squeeze in.

"Oh my God," Ralph said. He turned and ran for help.

The boy lay face up on the linoleum floor, his frail frame lifeless, yet his eyes open. They were large hazel eyes in dark sockets. The eyes looked at Chuck, but there was no recognition, no expression in the hollow face. The boy was dehydrated. How long he had been locked in was uncertain, but his pajamas were half torn off and his legs were caked with dried excrement. Chuck picked him up and felt the body's limpness. The child must have been nearly three years old, Chuck thought, yet he seemed to have no weight, no substance. Chuck placed the child on the couch and stroked his head in a gesture of reassurance. Then Chuck heard the crying again. A baby moaning in sobs like a puppy. The sound came from the bedroom. Chuck looked to the bedroom door to see Jo-Jo coming out with the infant cradled in his arm. He, too, had the sunken hazel eyes, the excrement-caked body. Jo-Jo sat down on the floor and rocked the child in his massive arm. Jo-Jo was making soothing noises; the huge man's pocked cheeks were streaked with tears.

The ambulance arrived in about twenty minutes and took the children away. Jo-Jo didn't want to give the baby up at first, but Chuck told him that he could go to the hospital along with Jimmy, who was to handle all admission papers.

After they left, Chuck and Ralph stood in the room. They said nothing for several minutes. Chuck was bringing himself together, and he now, for the first time, was cognizant of the nauseating smell. Chuck looked at the wet spot on the lineoleum where the boy had lain. The jamb of the door was scratched, and he visualized the child pawing at the door like a puppy, until his fingers bled and his strength left him.

"How could she leave them?" Ralph said. Chuck didn't answer. "Only an animal would do such a thing, and then it would eat its young instead of lettin' 'em suffer. How can you stand these animals?"

Chuck didn't answer. Instead, he attempted a faint smile, then went into the bathroom and threw up. Chuck went straight home that night and spent hours holding his own children close to him.

79

# 6

Most of the night Chuck lay in bed with his eyes open. To close them was to invoke the image of the abandoned children, dying in their own squalor. His own children would superimpose themselves on the apartment, his Pepe caged in the crib, his Tony scratching at the door jamb. When his eyes were open, his mind became enveloped in a kaleidescopic review of his problems—no rents . . . student protesters . . . Anita's insecurity . . . and the children. His thoughts kept coming back to the children. His children. The city's children. Those kids had gotten to him, and that made Chuck mad at himself. Violence was as much a part of life here as the loud music, the prostitutes, the packs of wandering dogs. Chuck had learned to tune it all out. He could watch a man get his intestines ripped open at eleven-thirty and eat a hearty lunch at noon. He could pistol-whip a man one moment and be telling jokes to another the next. But somewhere deep in his primal instincts was the reflex to shelter the young, to perpetuate an inane species. When asked about his softness for kids, Chuck called it his "social concern" for children exposed to cruelty, perversion, and insensitivity, who would years hence be the pimps, the whores, the winos, the cop killers. Chuck knew it was true, but he also suspected that his underlying reason for protecting children was simply a gut-level feeling, a sensitivity he could do little to shake.

At eight A.M. the next morning Chuck found himself entering the Children's Hospital emergency room. There, sleeping across three antiseptic white chairs, was Jo-Jo. Chuck let him sleep and went on to the emergency desk. There was a middle-aged redhead at the desk writing on a chart. They're always writing on charts, Chuck thought, as he said:

"Morning. I'd like to find out what happened to a couple of babies brought in here last night. I don't have their names or anything, but they were brought in by that big fellow over there."

The nurse looked at Chuck with the blankness of a computer not yet registering, then something seemed to spark behind her glasses and she got up fast and scurried into an inner office. She came back just as rapidly, followed by a police sergeant.

"You related to those boys?" the policeman asked, in a way that sounded to Chuck like a threat.

"No, I own the building they lived in. How are they?"

"You got any information on the mother's whereabouts? A description? Is that deaf-mute related to the kids? He's been hanging around ever since they were brought in."

"He works for me. We found the kids, but that's all I know. You'll have to go over to the building to get the details on the mother, but she's probably found a loaded john and skipped town with him. Now, how are the kids?"

The police officer glanced at the nurse and nodded. She pulled out another chart, then looked at Chuck. "The infant is listed as critical but seems to be responding nicely to IV's and should be out of Intensive Care soon. The older child died at 3:52 this morning."

"Thank you," Chuck said. He went over and shook Jo-Jo by the shoulder. Jo-Jo sat up in an awkward motion that clanked the metal chairs against the tile wall. He rubbed his huge hands across his face several times, then looked up at Chuck for an explanation. Chuck gave Jo-Jo the OK sign with his hand, then fingered out the message that both boys were doing fine. There was nothing more to worry about. It was a lie, but one Chuck knew Jo-Jo could never discover. There are benefits, Chuck thought, to being deaf to the world.

82

A few minutes later, Chuck was driving north on the Lodge Freeway with Jo-Jo sitting alongside him. Chuck really didn't need Jo-Jo's help for the chore he was now going on, but he felt Jo-Jo needed the ride. Not that driving on the expressway was an outing. Chuck likened it to driving in a ditch. On surface streets there were people, even on a frigid November day; and there were building facades to scan, hanging gargoyles to psych you out. But in the expressway trench there were only embankments of gray-black snow and not even a curve to break the monotony. Yet here Chuck was driving in the ditch, because, like all of the commuters who channeled through it, the expressway was the fastest way to get to the suburbs. Chuck was in a hurry. He had made up his mind to move his family out of Detroit, to shelter his children. It was something he had to do, so, like pulling off a bandage, he wanted to get it over and done with.

Chuck watched the broad, flat hood of his Cadillac seem to steamroll down the fast lane. He held to the same lane, pushed hard on the throttle, and rode up close behind other bumpers until his presence unnerved one driver after another into getting out of his way. Chuck kept his mind on the motion and thought not at all of the direction. That was decided without thought, for, as he saw it, north was the only direction his house hunting could take. South of Detroit was Windsor, Ontario. Many Detroiters had moved to Windsor and commuted by tunnel or bridge across the river, but Windsor was Canada, and Chuck was a naturalized American and didn't like the idea of crossing international borders. West and southwest were equally out of the question, for west would bring him to Dearborn, and Chuck wanted no part of that. Dearborn was Ford Motor Company country. Though most of the company's workers were black or Mediterranean like himself, Dearborn's inhabitants were lily-white. Chuck didn't know how the city or the company, or both, managed to keep the great unwashed masses out. He didn't care to know, but that exclusive club wasn't for him. Below Dearborn were the down-river communities that also were downwind from Detroit's industrial area. Rimming the east were the Grosse Pointes, where the muckymucks resided. Too rich for his blood. Not that snobs didn't move north, too—Birmingham was north. Nor that there weren't bigot centers north,

83

for Warren was north as well. But scattered between those communities there were places left that Costa considered unpretentious. If he had to retreat from the city, he at least could find such a spot.

Chuck drove with one eye on the brown-gray cloud above him. Scud, a mixture of smoke, clouds, and airborne garbage, hung like a dome overhead. After a half hour when he finally drove out from under the scud dome, Chuck pulled off the expressway. He was in Livonia, as good a suburb as any to begin house hunting. With the help of a local newspaper Chuck picked a half dozen BY OWNER house ads. The closest was in an area called Oak Trails Subdivision. False advertising, he concluded, as he drove into the subdivision and realized that Oak Trails had no oak trees, unless the gangly twigs spiked up on every other snow-blanketed lawn were infant oaks. The saplings, the yards, and the dwellings were all about two years old, and as near as Chuck could judge, all from the same litter. He stopped in front of a brick ranch whose lone distinction was a FOR SALE sign next to the door. Chuck left Jo-Jo in the car, then went up and knocked.

The woman who answered the door was attractive. She wore long thin-lined slacks that accentuated her height. She seemed uncertain, nervous about letting a man in to inspect. Chuck applied a few indicators that he was anxious to buy, then let greed do its work in overcoming her apprehensions. The house was well laid out, well designed, but there the quality stopped. Chuck inspected the window frames and found them mismatched and off-mitered. Plasterboard walls, plywood flooring, Chuck thought as he went from room to room complimenting the woman on the wallpaper and furnishings. The glass wall onto a patio was set a quarter inch off, enough to allow cold air in and run up a heating bill.

The woman grew tired of Chuck's thorough inspection and excused herself to go to the kitchen as Chuck inspected the basement plumbing. He was shaking his head at all of the plastic pipes when he heard the scream, a horror-stricken scream coming from the kitchen.

"Get him away from me," the woman screamed. Chuck entered the kitchen and saw her standing with a butcher knife in hand and her back against the turquoise refrigerator door. And there before her was Jo-Jo.

84

He was grunting loud, motioning with his hands to the woman, trying to explain. But she was terrified, and began to scream again.

"It's all right," Chuck said. He came between them. "He's with me." Chuck asked Jo-Jo what happened. He answered with such rapid hand motions that Chuck had difficulty following, and the woman's continued screaming didn't help his understanding either. But Chuck got the gist of it. Jo-Jo had to go to the bathroom, so he came up to the house, and since the door was ajar, entered. The woman had her back to the door when Jo-Jo entered. He grunted acknowledgment. She screamed and threw the batter she was mixing at him. Jo-Jo was flustered and tried to explain. Chuck told Jo-Jo to go back to the car.

"But the bathroom," Jo-Jo said with his hands.

"All right. Go, then get back to the car." Chuck talked to the woman for another twenty minutes for no other good reason than to calm her. Even asking how much cash she wanted for the house didn't bring her back down. Finally, Chuck left the woman. She was still clinging to the carving knife. All the way back into the city Chuck kept thinking about the house. Poor quality, drab, and expensive. He could buy ten times as much house in the inner city for a quarter the price. Is this what people were escaping to? He didn't understand why. Perhaps there was a security in the sameness of the streets, and of the people. Certainly there was an order, a uniformity about it all that might spell security. Chuck wanted no part of it and at that moment was glad that his appointment with Peter Balantine had kept him from seeing more of suburbia.


For the first time in three weeks, Peter Balantine stopped his car in front of 1406 Temple, the apartment building that he and his mother owned. Today was the day it would happen, either Costa would win out, or Peter would be out of business entirely. Peter sat in his Volkswagen for several minutes wishing he had taken a tranquilizer before leaving home. He was frightened and he knew it. Not of the tenants, but of one small girl. She would be there at the tenants' meeting. She would hear bad things said about this "slumlord." She would remember how he was humiliated. Peter didn't want to see her, even though she had

85

crowded most of his thoughts for several weeks. Maybe she had moved, he thought, but then started wondering how he could find her in such a large, anonymous city. Peter was startled by a knock on his car window. It was Chuck Costa.

"Let's go," Chuck said. "The lions are waiting inside."

Peter turned off the engine and stepped out into a gust of wind that momentarily stole his breath. Then both men ran into the brownstone building.

A mass of black faces greeted them in the basement laundry area, the only room in the building large enough to hold a tenants' meeting. The mumble of the crowd raised appreciably as several people shouted hellos to "Charles" and "Chuck" and "Mr. Costa." Peter saw Sheila's pale face on the opposite side of the basement. She was sitting on an automatic washer, staring directly at him. He felt a surge of adrenalin, a rising and dashing of emotion.

Chuck went headlong into the middle of the crowd, shaking hands and making asides to several people. He acted like a politician, Peter thought. Why, he seems to know more of my tenants than I do.

"Let's call this meeting to order," a lanky black man said. He was standing on the second step, using it as a platform. Chuck leaned over to Peter and whispered that the man was Jesse Coleman from the Temple Street Tenants' Association, the group that supported his apartment building's rent strike.

"Quiet it down back there," Coleman said. "There. That's better. Now, you all know why this meeting was called. Chuck Costa asked that we try and straighten this rat hole out."

"Amen," came the response from several sectors.

"Before I let Chuck tell us just what he has in mind, I'd like to say that I've known this man for damn near ten years, and I ain't once caught him talking honky shit."

"Amen," came from at least two people in the crowd.

"So let's let the man say what he came for."

Chuck went up and took Coleman's spot on the second step. Peter didn't know just where he should be standing, but he finally decided that the foot of the stairs, off to one side was about right. He could see Sheila clearly from his new vantage point.

86

"I'm here because I don't want to see this building boarded up," Chuck said. "I know you had some problems with Mr. Balantine, but that's past now. Let's forget it and fix the place up real nice again."

"But things ain't right," one woman yelled out. "Someone's been victimized here."

"Yes, ma'am, someone has," Chuck said. "But tell me, who?"

"My sink is off the wall," another woman yelled.

"OK, we'll fix it. But who must replace that sink? The landlord, right? Who must pay the violation from the city? The landlord. Who tore the sink out? You did, lady, so who's the victim?"

The crowd began making more noise. Peter thought Chuck was about to lose them.

"What I'm saying," Chuck said (his voice was two octaves higher now), "is that you had your share in this problem. But we'll fix it. I've got a crew of men ready to move in this afternoon to fix every last problem. But you got to have pride in the place, you got to keep it up."

"My heater don't work," someone yelled.

"You got a man around, honey?" Chuck asked.

"No."

"No wonder you're cold." The crowd laughed. "We'll fix your heater, but you'll have to find your own man."

"The rent's too high," someone else said.

"Does it make any difference?" Chuck said. "You ain't paying it anyhow. But if you don't start paying, you're going out the door. I promise you this place will be nice. But I can't carry no loafers. Now I know you all withheld rents, so you're a month behind and don't have the money. OK, we'll clean the slate. Forget that month; it's a gift from Mr. Balantine and me for your inconvenience. But today rent starts again. If it don't start, you get out. It's that simple. I'll board this place up tomorrow, if I can't make any money. And Mr. Coleman will tell you I mean it."

The crowd fell quiet. No one spoke. They looked at Costa. He stared back at them. Peter expected a fight. Then Jesse Coleman got up on the first step. "If Chuck boards this place up, where you gonna go next?" he said. "There ain't many buildings left that ain't fullover. Now I know Chuck Costa does what he says. Let's go along with him."

Heads started bobbing in affirmation throughout the crowd.

"One more thing," Chuck said. "Peter Balantine is the new general manager for all of my buildings." Peter couldn't believe what Chuck was saying. They had not talked about his coming to work for Chuck. Not once.

"Mr. Balantine made some mistakes here. But he's learned what he did wrong, and now that he's working for me, you can bet he won't make any next time." No one answered. "When the men come this afternoon, you show them just what needs fixing. Mr. Balantine will be in charge, and if those workmen don't do it right, you talk to him. He told me he's going to stay right here in the building until everything is in perfect order again. Now go on out and spend last month's rent money, if you haven't already done it."

Chuck stepped down into the basement, clearing the way for people to go up. They were talking loud, some laughing, a few with arms still crossed. Peter edged his way in next to Chuck.

"What's this general manager talk?" he whispered.

"I need help right now. The job pays eight hundred a month," Chuck said, then he walked away to talk to Coleman. Peter was thoroughly confused. He waited until Coleman left to get at Chuck again.

"But . . . but what about the month's back rent you just gave away?"

"You never would have gotten that anyway. This way, we look like heroes for writing it off. You'll make it up, if they start paying. If they don't, it won't make much difference."

Another cluster enveloped Costa, and Peter backed away. He wasn't sure if he had won or lost yet, but at least he was back in charge. Then Peter remembered Sheila. He looked toward the washer; she was still sitting on top of it. Her thin legs dangled in an absentminded rhythm that drew Peter's eye. He wanted to talk to her now. Chuck came over.

"I've got to get back to work," Chuck said. "Court this afternoon. You stay around. Georgie and the cleanup crew will be in later on. Get into those rooms with them and make some points with these people. Tomorrow you can start collecting at my buildings."

Chuck left, and Peter found himself gravitating toward Sheila. She smiled as he neared. Her legs stopped swinging.

"Hi, Peter."

"Hi."

"General managers don't have much time to come around," she said.

Peter was close now. He could smell her perfume. Her powder. She seemed to wear more of both than his mother did. "That's not why I haven't come around. It was the rent strike. I just didn't feel I could."

"Got time for coffee?"

Peter suddenly felt good. "Sure, didn't you hear Chuck say I've got to stay put until the place is all fixed up?"

"That could take forever."

"Only if I'm lucky."

Sheila's apartment was a studio, with a kitchenette and a living room with a hidden Murphy bed behind a door. Since she was such a petite girl, probably not more than five feet, he figured, the apartment seemed fitting. Like a doll house for a miniature person. Peter familiarized himself with the front room again as Sheila was busied in the kitchen making coffee. The room was decidedly feminine. Everything that wasn't ruffled seemed to be crocheted or embroidered. There were lots of colors, all soft like her. Pastels of every shade, so much in such a small room that much of it seemed to compete. Peter also felt he was invading a child's room because of all the stuffed bears and carnival Kewpie dolls. Sheila had once told him that she was madly in love with circuses, and the room confirmed it. Yet somehow Peter felt that it all made sense. It all fit Sheila's delicate and exciting nature.

Peter was sitting on the couch as she entered. She put his coffee down on the end table, then stood looking down at him. Neither spoke. Peter felt no need for words. Before they would talk for hours on end, but the lapse of three weeks had done something to their relationship. They both seemed to know this. Peter reached out and toyed with the hem of her dress. She placed one of her hands on his hair and began to stroke him gently. He moved his hands up to her hips. They were firm and pronounced. Peter rubbed them. Sheila placed both hands on his head and pulled him against her. His face came up against her abdomen. He could feel her body tighten. Her thighs were no larger than his hand. Soft and warm.

Sheila stepped back away from him. For a moment he thought she

89

was rejecting him. Then he watched her reach up and unzip the dress and let it fall around her ankles. She stood motionless with only her silken underpants on. Her breasts were small and upthrust. The nipples were dark and hard. Peter pulled her back against him. As he kissed her, he reached up and caressed her breasts. Their tongues caressed one another's. Sheila reached down and began to undo his trousers. She was nervous, clumsy. Peter helped her with the snap. He put her on the couch and began kissing her. "Oh, Peter," she said, her voice panicked, "please, take me now."

Peter stayed on the couch with Sheila most of the afternoon. The couch was too short for him, so he had to curl up around her, holding her, stroking her. The sun streamed in through the window. Peter wished it was night. He could hear the workmen banging at pipes and woodwork and knew he should be with them, but he didn't want to move; not now, not ever. It had all come together at once, the apartment, Sheila; and he felt that if he moved, he would fall from his pinnacle. Sheila moved away finally. She made him coffee, lit him a cigarette, and slowly brought him back down to a point where his sense of duty took over. Peter went to help the workmen.

Slumlord Costa talks with tenants. One of his constant problems
is to discourage public drinking on steps of his buildings.

Charles Costa paid bounty on rats to encourage slum dwellers to kill them. Here he is shown holding one of his "rat reward" signs.

Costa's repair crew goes to work to fix up
multi-family building in Detroit's inner city.

Costa shows bathroom vandalized by tenants.
Such costly damage is one reason many owners of
slum buildings simply give up and walk away.

Television reporter interviews Costa.
Slumlord's fight to maintain decent housing in inner city
has gained him wide attention from the local press.

Costa stands proudly before an inner city
apartment complex he rehabilitated.

# 7

The statue sat cross-legged on his marble pedestal in front of the City-County Building. He was the symbol of Detroit, holding the sun in one upthrust hand and the family of man in the palm of the other. The eyes of the monument spoke of benevolence as they peered down on the miniature people in hand. Snow was falling, filling up the hand and cloaking the naked, green-marble shoulders of the statue. Chuck glanced up at the figure as he passed into the building. He didn't like the symbol. To him it represented an image of the city, or perhaps of God, that irked him. Incompetent little creatures, secure in the palm of an all-compassionate caretaker. But this afternoon Chuck had no time to think about the handout image, and he passed it by with the thought that the damned fool statue might freeze its brass rear end off sitting out in the cold.

On the eighth floor Ralph O'Hara was pacing the tiles as Chuck approached. "You're late for court," Ralph said.

"Uh-huh. What's on the agenda?"

Ralph shook his head and began thumbing through the briefcase he held open before him. "I went to a lot of trouble to get you the same court date for both building violations and the burglary thing, and now you might be too late for—"

"Let's just go in, Ralph," Chuck said. He pushed through the double doors into the mumbling crowd in the tenant courtroom. One black man in the back row of chairs brought his eyes up at Chuck and grinned. It was Raymond, the man he had caught stripping the John R. building. Alongside Raymond was a young black with a leg in a cast. Chuck couldn't remember the face but figured that it was the man he had shot.

"Mr. Costa, you're late," the judge said over the heads of a plaintiff and a defendant who stood at the bench.

"Sorry, your honor. I was held up."

"Well, I hope they didn't steal your wallet; you've got three citations in front of this court today'" the judge said. That's Lazinski for you, Chuck thought, always half joking, even when he handed down stiff fines.

"No, your honor, they didn't take my wallet. It was already empty."

"If the court pleases," Ralph broke in, "my client would like to beg the court's pardon for being late and ask that our cases be heard now."

"The court doesn't so please, Mr. O'Hara. This court isn't late, your client is. So you tell me your client has to leave early to make up for coming in late."

"But Judge Lazinski, my client was inadvertently detained in—"

"I know, Mr. O'Hara; we've gone through that already. Disregarding my docket order, I'll hear your case out of order. But this is the last time, Mr. Costa, I will bend this court's scheduling for you."

"Thanks, your honor," Chuck said. He was sure the others in the courtroom were giving him the hard eye, as if he had just taken cuts into a ticket line.

The judge leafed through papers on his desk, and O'Hara did the same thing in front of the desk. The building was overheated, and Chuck was getting impatient to be out already.

"First violation is 438 Myrtle," Lazinski said. He handed a piece of paper down to the court reporter sitting at a small table with a scroll-spewing machine in front of her. "Three violations: plugged sewage pipe in Apartment 5B, refuse on the premises, and mailboxes in disrepair. Have these violations been rectified?"

"Yes, sir. Or at least they were yesterday when I was over there.

100

Your honor, these citations were not my doing. I can't stop tenants from trying to flush a dead fetus down the toilet. I can't clean up for them."

"The inspector notes here that he issued this citation for garbage in the yard on November fifteen. On November twenty-four he came to the premises again, and the yard still contained refuse."

"That yard was cleaned up after your inspector was out. But the people in that place airmail their garbage, right out the window every time."

"Then I suggest you get a net to catch it," the judge said. "That count will be a $250 fine or thirty days. Now, what about the mailboxes?"

"Sir," O'Hara broke in. "I'd like to point out to the court that there has been a rash of mailbox burglaries in the last month, ever since the state legislature passed the law sending rent money directly to welfare recipients. It has become virtually impossible for my client to keep mailboxes in repair."

A dozen people in the gallery made sounds of agreement, which brought the judge's gavel down. "If someone walks off with the roof, Mr. O'Hara, that is still a violation of the building code."

"The repairs have been made to those boxes," Chuck said. He was beginning to add some heat of his own to the stuffy courtroom. "And the fetus was taken out of the john, so it's fixed, too."

"Fine," the judge said. "Now if you will pay the bailiff, we can get on with the next case you are involved in. For the record, this will be *The City of Detroit* versus *Raymond Smith and James Bower*. Are the attorneys in this case present?"

Chuck pulled a wad of money from his front pocket and leafed off five fifty-dollar bills onto the bailiff's table. His eyes, however, were on the two suited men coming forward from the corner of the court. He had noticed them whispering together when he came in, but now he recognized them. One was from the prosecuting attorney's office and the other from the free legal clinic. Chuck had seen them in court before and marvelled that neither looked old enough to shave. At the same time, a guard from somewhere behind the bench pushed out a shopping cart filled with pieces of copper piping. There was a red tag on one of the pieces. Chuck felt good at seeing all the evidence of the burglary present to support his case.

"Yes, your honor," one of the two young lawyers said, "we are ready. And at this time I would like to offer a plea of guilty to a reduced charge of attempted burglary for both of my clients."

"Attempted?" Chuck broke in. "What attempted? Those men ripped out my plumbing. That plumbing sitting right there in that cart."

"Mr. Costa," the judge said, "you're out of order."

"No, sir, I'm in order. This court's out of order. The evidence is right here." Chuck picked up a piece of copper pipe and tossed it onto the bench. The judge jerked backward. "These lawyers can't be making deals when we got evidence and an eye witness."

"Mr. Costa, that outburst will cost you one hundred dollars in contempt of court. Mr. O'Hara, if you don't restrain your client. . . ."

"Yes, sir," Ralph said, popping up beside Chuck and gripping his arm as if to restrain him. Chuck looked at Ralph and felt disgust, then pulled his arm away.

"Judge, you know this ain't right," Chuck said. "Those men destroyed my property. You give them a reduced charge, and they'll be back next week ripping landlords off again."

"Perhaps you'd like to try for a two-hundred-dollar fine, Mr. Costa. According to the record, that building was substandard already. A slum, Mr. Costa. Should this court send two young men to five years in prison for burglarizing an empty building that belongs to a slumlord?"

Chuck instinctively flushed and moved toward the judge. He grabbed the railing with both hands to keep his hands from reaching for the judge. "Landlords don't make slums, Lazinski. But slums make slumlords. Courts without respect for property make slums, not slumlords."

"Attendant," the judge called out, leaning back in his chair as if to put more distance between Costa and himself, "attendant, remove this man from the courtroom—after you've relieved him of another two hundred dollars for contempt of court."

"Two hundred," Chuck said. "That's a bargain price on the contempt I've got. A real bargain."

Chuck gave his money to O'Hara, then turned to walk out with the attendant a step behind him. But there was Raymond sitting in the back row, sprawled over his chair and grinning. Chuck stopped and looked down at him. He wanted to smash his face in, hand down an immediate

102

sentence that the court was too weak to deliver. But Chuck was too mad even to strike. He stood staring down at Raymond, who, feeling the threat, sat up and swallowed his grin. The attendant pushed Chuck from behind, and, deciding it wasn't worth going to jail over, Chuck walked out.

"Mr. Costa," a voice from behind called out as Chuck headed for the elevator. He pushed the button without looking back, then felt a gentle hand on his sleeve. "Mr. Costa," the voice said, and Chuck looked at the miniature man behind it. He was about five feet tall, bent over as if carrying a trunk. His slightly bowed head was gray, as were the spikes of a beard that stood out against his deep brown cheeks.

"I'm sorry," Costa said, "I'm in a hurry."

"Mr. Costa, I seen you in there. You stood up to that judge, and . . . ."

"Look, I'm really in a hurry."

"Mr. Costa, we need you. I'm a landlord too. Oh, I only got a couple of buildings, but I saved up twenty years in the Rouge plant to get them for retirement. They aren't paying."

"Move over," Chuck said. "Every landlord in this town has the same problem. I can't help you."

"Sure you kin. I've gotten a few landlords like me together. We want to organize and get things made better. You could lead us."

"I'm no politician."

"But you get things done," the old man said as he pulled a fistful of newspaper clippings out of his coat pocket. "Last year you got the garbage charge turned down by yourself. You make news. People listen. Why, in today's paper they call you 'Chuck Costa, the Rat Man,' and they say because of you Detroit's going to get a fifty-thousand dollar federal grant for rat control."

"Let me see that," Chuck said. He took the paper and read the front-page article.

"If you were leading us, Mr. Costa, they'd listen."

Chuck handed the man back his paper. "Thank you. I'll have to get a copy. How many landlords have you gotten together?"

"Keep the paper. We only got ten people so far, but with you we could get more."

Ralph came up alongside and stood by the old man, and Chuck realized from the glances they exchanged that his lawyer had set him up for this encounter.

"There are probably a couple thousand landlords in this town," Chuck said. "Speaking for ten wouldn't carry any weight."

"You could get more."

Chuck pushed the elevator button again. "I don't think so. Most landlords don't even join the Book-of-the-Month Club because it's too confining. They're loners. I've tried to get them together twice before, and got no takers. No way."

"But now," Ralph broke in, "they have more reason to organize. This new law is going to strangle all of you, Chuck."

Chuck stepped into the elevator. It was packed. Ralph started to come in after him, but Chuck pushed him back out and smiled. "I'll think about it," Chuck said. The doors slid closed.


Ten minutes later Chuck was back at his office. He had calmed enough to enter through the waiting room and nod at the half a dozen managers waiting around the room. The men seemed more solemn than they used to, and Chuck knew it was because they were here to report that they couldn't collect all of the rent. He had been hearing the story daily. The direct payment to welfare tenants meant at least a fifty percent loss of rents. Chuck was in no mood to hear it now. He went straight into his office and closed the door. Marilyn was on the telephone. He went to the desk and picked up the stack of messages. There were three from the electric company. Marilyn hung up the phone.

"What's the electric company want?" he asked.

"I guess they want their money," Marilyn said. She seemed worried. "We didn't have enough in the account last week to send them a check. The rents aren't coming in to cover overhead."

Chuck sat down in the nearest chair. He sat on the edge and leaned forward, staring at the carpet. Then he realized that he might be adding to Marilyn's worries. "Hey," he said. "That's no problem. I've got a couple of big shots coming down to buy the Temple Street building next week. We'll sell that one and pay that stuff off. Don't get up-tight about it. Did you start calling around to fill those Christmas baskets?"

104

"I didn't think you could afford it this year," she said. "I didn't believe you'd want them."

"Come on, Merl, we're not on welfare yet. I've put those Christmas baskets out for the kids for six years. You don't want me to have to play Scrooge?"

"Yes, sir, I guess we could charge it. But what if the building doesn't sell?"

Chuck got up and beamed. "Then I'll send Jo-Jo out to rob a bank. I mean, if money is our only trouble . . . ."

Suddenly there was the shattering of glass, the thud of something striking the desk. Marilyn fell back, reaching for her face. Before Chuck knew what had happened, he saw the blood on Marilyn's forehead and leaped across the desk to catch her before she hit the floor. Someone had thrown a rock through the window, had struck Marilyn.

"You all right?" he asked as he sat her in the typing chair and brushed her black hair back away from the injury. She was bleeding, but it was only a trickle. He felt a hand on his shoulder and saw Anita come from nowhere with the first-aid kit. Anita took over, and Chuck stood up. All of the managers were inside the door gawking. Chuck felt a rush of icy air cross his face and looked to the broken window. He looked outside. No one was on the street.

"Don't stand there," he said to the managers, "get outside and find out who threw that rock."

"I'm fine," Marilyn said. She made a gesture to get up from the chair, but Anita gently motioned her down. Anita cleansed the cut and bandaged it. Anita's expression as she worked on the wound was stoic, but the color in her face was gone. Chuck sensed that she was as injured as Merl.

Georgie came into the room fast. He stopped short of Chuck and gasped for breath to speak. "Someone just blew up the Cass Avenue building. Just heard it on the police call radio."

"Can you handle this?" Chuck said to Anita. She nodded. "OK, let's go, Georgie."

Smoke was rising and curling up under the clouds as Chuck neared the area. There were crowds in the street, people standing on top of cars to get a look. Chuck and Georgie left the car a block away and pushed through the people on foot. A number of fire engines obscured Chuck's view of the building as he half ran toward it. The fire hoses spread like snakes in a pit over the entire area; the pavement was an inch deep in water. The hoses, the water, let off steam in the brittle cold air. Chuck stopped as soon as he could see what had happened. The bottom floor of his building was gone, pushed out as if a bulldozer had come out through the wall. There was no recognizable sign of the bar that had been in that spot. Smoke continued to pour out of the hole in the building, and firemen rushed about it like a battalion of penguins. About fifty feet away Chuck recognized the small group of people huddling together, some wrapped in fire blankets. They were his tenants, and he could see by their blank expressions that they were in shock. Chuck moved toward them.

"Sorry, buddy," a police officer said, "this area is off limits."

"My name's Costa. I own that building."

"Or what's left of it," the cop said. He smiled so frankly that Chuck couldn't help but return it in kind.

"Was anyone hurt?"

"I don't think so," the policeman said. "The explosion was pretty much limited to the bar. It was empty, I was told."

"Yes," Chuck said. "The leasees were reworking the place."

"Everyone says we got all the tenants out," the officer said. He waved at a cop on the other side of the street. "It's lucky it happened around dinner time when everyone was awake and dressed."

Chuck's feet were cold. He realized he had been standing in a puddle. "What happened? Do you know yet?"

"Some guy was seen throwing something in the door. Not much of a description, an average-size Caucasian wearing one of those green jackets. One witness thought it looked like a Wayne State University jacket. Anyways, it was probably a bomb of some kind. Crazy, huh? Doesn't make too much sense to bomb a vacant bar."

"Look, officer. Those people are my tenants. I'd like to move them into one of my other buildings. Get them out of the cold. Could some of your men help transport them a few blocks?"

"Well," the cop said. He took his hat off and rubbed his hair back. "I'll have to get the sergeant over here for that. What's your name again?"

"Costa. Chuck Costa. Why don't you get him now? It's too damn

106

cold for these people to be out here." Chuck walked away from the officer, and Georgie followed. They stepped carefully over hoses and around equipment to get to the small band of tenants.

"All right," Chuck said. He pushed into the center of the group. "Which one of you passed gas and blew my building all to hell?"

"That's not funny, Chuck," one tenant said.

"I know it's not, Sam, but it was the best I could do on the spur of the moment." Chuck rubbed a few heads and tried as best he could to feign a smile. "Hey, if you promise not to do that again, I've got another building about three blocks from here about half vacant. Most of the apartments are furnished."

"I already bought all my Christmas presents," one stocky woman said.

"And all of our clothes," someone else joined. In a moment everyone started talking, complaining. A few even crying.

"Hold it. Hold it a minute." Chuck raised his hand. "First thing is to get in out of the cold. Then we'll get some social service people out. Some Salvation Army people for clothes." Chuck saw the police sergeant coming over. I'm in luck, he thought. It's Joe Polanski. The policeman stopped on the outer ring of the group and nodded his head at Chuck. He was pointing, and Chuck looked in that direction and saw a large red paddy wagon, big enough to carry the lot in a single trip.

"You people go with Sergeant Polanski there. Georgie, you go with them and set them up at the Beaubien Street building. Call all the do-gooders to get some food and clothes out to them," Chuck said. He then took a step closer in to Georgie and gave the remainder of his instructions in Greek. "Find that blond girl from Wayne. She's got to be behind this. You have the crew, find her; I'll do the rest. Understand?"

"We'll find her," Georgie said in Greek.

Chuck threaded his way back through the maze of fire equipment, hoses, water, and onlookers, back to his car. A kid was standing on the hood of his Eldorado to get a better view of the action. Chuck banged his hand on the fender, and the boy jumped off. Chuck slid in behind the wheel, and was about to insert the key, when he noticed the radio was gone; wires dangled out of the rectangular chasm it left. The glove compartment door was standing open. Nothing was missing from that. He sat back and was about to start again, when he saw in the rearview mirror that his trunk was slightly open. He got out and inspected. The trunk lock had been popped; the spare tire was gone. Well, at least they didn't steal the motor, Chuck thought as he started the car and headed for home.

By the time he got back to the office, it was dark. Chuck went in through the front, through the vacant outer office, and into his own office. From the streetlight through the window he could see the cardboard over the missing pane and the white lid of the first-aid kit still sitting on the floor. A feeling of uselessness, of utter exhaustion came over him. he sat down in the armchair, not to think, but to bring himself back up before he went in the house. The hall door opened, sending out a carpet runner of light across the room and up to the foot of his chair. Anita's silhouette appeared. Chuck didn't get up. She crossed over to him, then sat at his feet, just as the children did when he told them stories of the old country. Chuck reached out and grabbed a handful of her hair. It felt soft to the touch, warm in the palm of his cold right hand. "How's Merl?" he whispered.

"She went home about an hour ago. The rock only glanced off her head, but it scared her."

"Yeh, I know. Did anyone see who did it?"

"They said it was a bearded boy and a blond-haired girl. Police said they think they were from Wayne State University."

"I know the girl. She's flipped out on social injustice."

"Marilyn's dad called and said she can't work for you anymore," Anita said. She, too, spoke in a whisper.

"That's all right. Another week or two and I'd be paying her salary in buildings anyhow."

Anita laid her head on his leg and turned her face up toward him. "Is it that bad?"

"Not really," Chuck said. He said it much louder and firmer than his earlier words. Once said, he wondered if Anita would catch the excessive emphasis. "I'll have to sell off a couple of buildings to get by, but it's been rough before. Nothing I can't handle." Chuck stroked her hair and wished to himself he could have sounded more convincing.

# 8

Vendettas take time, a commodity Chuck had precious little of during the next three weeks. He had to find buyers for some of his buildings, quick cash to pay the mortgage payments, and time was running out. He had to find a house in suburbia for Anita, who had become more determined than ever to move after the rock throwing. He had to train Peter Balantine as general manager at a time when he himself didn't know of a sure way to collect rents. He had to keep ahead of the vandalism in his buildings—windows, doors, plumbing, and mailboxes, all being ripped out or ripped off daily. And then there was the demand of Christmas, family time, and that just a week away. No, there was no time for a vendetta against Susan Stanicki, the blond leader of the Wayne radicals. She had stoned his office, had his building bombed, and Chuck was determined that she would pay. But after the incidents, she had blended into the campus broth, and Chuck's men didn't have the right ingredients to follow her in. She would pay, he said to himself, but right now there just wasn't time.

More important, Chuck had lined up two buyers for two of his buildings, and today he was sure he would clinch the deal. In the past three weeks he had advertised his buildings for sale in the major newspapers, and had gotten plenty of calls, but once the locations of the buildings were determined, there was an invariable hesitation on the other end of the line, and finally a polite "thanks, but no thanks." This morning it was going to be different. He was going to meet the pair of buyers and escort them to the buildings, and firm up the sales. If he could sell off two, he could save them all. The buyers, brothers from Grosse Pointe named Goldsmith, were anxious to buy. They were not, however, anxious to enter the buildings. Chuck had assured them it was safe. They didn't buy that. Only after Chuck suggested meeting at the police station and going through with a police escort, did the Goldsmiths relent to looking over a couple of buildings.

On the way over to the first building, Chuck rode in the back of the police car with the Goldsmith brothers. The two officers made quips up front.

"That sure is a mean neighborhood you want to buy into, Mr. Goldsmith," one of the officers said. Chuck saw him wink at his partner behind the wheel. "Why, it was last night, wasn't it, Mike, when we had the shooting run to the building next door?"

"Yeah," the driver said.

"A couple of johns from the suburbs had been done in by murphy men. Christ, was that one a mess."

"Ah . . . what is a murphy man?" one of the Goldsmiths asked.

"A con man," Chuck said. "Harmless cons. They play pimps, take a guy's money, then send him up to a room that's empty, except for a Murphy bed."

"Not this time," the cop said. "These murphy men weren't satisfied with a couple of bills from the pimp act. They had four studs laying for the johns behind the door. Smashed them up good."

"Yeah," the other officer confirmed.

"Mean. Jesus. One of the johns about lost a finger because the guy who was beating on him couldn't get a diamond ring off fast enough, so he cut the finger near off to get the ring."

Chuck could feel one of the Goldsmiths squirm. He knew the cops were having a little fun with these obviously petrified money men, but their fun could cost him the sale.

"Come off it, you guys," Chuck said. "That cut-off-the-finger-to-get-the-ring story has whiskers on it. If you're going to tell scare stories, come up with some new material."

110

"OK," the officer said . He was grinning broadly now. "How about two days old? That's when some hillbilly got sick of his kids and tossed them out of the third-story window. That was right next door to the building you're headed for. One kid landed on the garbage cans and lived, but the one-year-old went *kersplat,* right on the pavement. What a mess that was to scrape up, right Mike?"

"Yeah."

Chuck couldn't argue with that tale, since he had read a less graphic rendition in yesterday's paper and had noted the building's proximity to his own. The cop was looking as if he had another horror story to spin when the car finally came to rest at the curb. The police got out, Chuck got out, but the Goldsmiths didn't budge from the back seat.

"Maybe we'll take your word for the building's condition," one of the brothers said. "Since your records and receipts are in order, there's no need to—"

"Nonsense," Chuck said. "There is absolutely nothing to be afraid of. Why, this is one of my quietest buildings. And we have two policemen along. What could possibly go wrong?"

"Cold policemen," the talkative cop said. "You guys want to look at this building, or you gonna freeze our asses off?"

Reluctantly, the Goldsmith brothers slid over to the door and came out. They, too, were shivering, but Chuck suspected that it was more of an inner chill with them. All five men started up the steps. Chuck was continuing to make reassuring noises, when it happened. The front door swung open and a man ran out. A butcher knife protruding from the middle of his chest. The man was yelling, "That bitch, that dirty bitch!" Blood covered his white T-shirt. The policemen grabbed the man, one on each arm, and he seemed to collapse into their arms, still muttering, "That dirty bitch."

"Chuck," the cop said, "we've got to run this man to General."

"Good, I'll go inside and call the hospital to let them know you're bringing him in." Chuck went in to make the call. As he dialed, he could hear the police car's siren whirring away. He finished the call and lit up a Chesterfield before he remembered that the Goldsmith brothers were not with him, and he knew the police wouldn't have taken them on an emergency run. Chuck went back out on the porch. The two small men were still on the steps, shivering beneath their heavy gray overcoats, yet

111

not moving from the spot where they were when the stabbed man had come out.

"The police are gone," one of the Goldsmiths said.

"That's OK, we don't need them to go in and look around."

"No, the police are gone and I don't really think we want to see any more. We've got to get back to our office."

They started down the street at a fast pace. Chuck walked along with them and tried to talk them out of it. "Look, we can come back later with some more fuzz. This is an excellent building, a bargain."

"I'm afraid we aren't interested in it right now, Mr. Costa. With stabbings . . . violence . . . I think I can speak for my brother in saying we're not interested."

Chuck stepped out in front of them and stopped them with outstretched arms. "All right. This might be too rough an area for you, but I've got another building that I think you'll like. It's safe. Over on John R. I can show it to you later."

The brothers looked at each other, then looked past Chuck's outstretched arms toward Woodward Avenue two blocks away. He knew they wanted to get to Woodward; that was the main street, and safety. If he held them up for a moment, they'd have to agree to seeing another building.

"Sure," Goldsmith finally said. "We'll look at another building, but it has to be a quiet one."

"No problem. I've got an excellent manager in my John R. building. A real good woman. You won't have to worry about anything."

"Shall we say four this afternoon?" Goldsmith said.

"Perfect," Chuck said. He dropped his arms and let the men escape.

There was no way of Chuck's knowing it, but things were not going perfectly at the John R. building that morning. Mrs. Brown was having a fight with her boyfriend, Sam.

"Everyone saw you was there with that hussy," she yelled, loud enough to drown out the soap opera on the television set, and louder than the music that forever penetrated the walls from tenants on all sides. "You can't go sleeping with them hussies and come back to get onto me."

112

Martin Luther listened to his mother from under his bed. He had taken refuge there when Sam came in an hour ago, and his mamma had started the screaming. Martin listened for Sam to argue back, to do something mean, but there was no noise from him. Once he peeked out to see if Sam was still there, or if he had just upped and left and his mamma was too mad to stop yelling. But he was there, sitting at the kitchen table, drinking a can of Stroh's beer and acting kind of bored with all the commotion. Martin now lay belly-up under the bed, holding his .45-caliber pistol and imagining what he'd have to do if Sam got rough with his mamma. The pistol was as large as Martin's face. He held it inches away from his nose to see it. There was no way to hold it at more of a distance with the bed springs as close in on him as they were.

"You no-good nigger," he heard his mamma say. "I'm running this apartment house and nobody's paying me, and I got troubles with thieves tearing the mailboxes off the front, and alls you do, alls you do is come around and drink my beer, so's you'll be high 'nough to honeymoon some hussy."

Martin Luther heard a crash. He slithered out from under the bed to where he could see Mamma and Sam in the kitchen. Mamma was smacking her hand on the table and cussing low under her breath. Finally, she snatched Sam's beer up from under his face and tossed it on the floor. The can hit on the bottom, and beer gushed up out of the tab hole like a water fountain. Sam got to his feet. He stood there. Not talking. Staring at Mamma. Martin stayed on his belly, but brought the gun up and aimed it at Sam's face. For an eternal moment nothing moved. Sam and Mamma stood looking hard at each other, neither noticing Martin lying low and keeping his gun pointed. Sam then walked over and opened the apartment door, looking back at Mamma. "Go f - - - yourself, woman," he said, and was gone before she could come at him.

Mrs. Brown began to wail and moan, like at a funeral, Martin Luther thought. She rocked back and forth and moaned. She was moaning low, and Martin could hear the audience roar on the TV as a contestant won a new refrigerator. Martin pushed the gun back under the bed and came out. She was bending down cleaning up the spilled beer. "Can I help with something, Mamma?" he asked. She waved him away and sat

113

down at the table. "Mamma, I can fix Sam good for you. I can do him with my —"

"No, child," she said. "Just go play in your room or something. Go away and leave me be." She drank the beer down and forcefully went to the refrigerator and got another. Martin went back to his room. His mamma was drinking beer, and he couldn't do anything. He knew she never did drink and that the few times when she would, she'd do strange things. She was best left alone if she was going to drink. Martin went back into his room and crawled back under his bed.

The morning didn't go much better for Peter Balantine as he made the rounds of Costa's buildings. He was supposed to be collecting rents, but all he was getting were excuses. "Didn't get my check," they'd say. "Someone stole it," they'd say. "Had to buy medicine," they'd say. "Just ain't got it, man. Catch you next time," they'd say. And all the while he had to strain to hear over the jive music on radios or TV's in every apartment. Kids and dogs would squeal or howl at his pant leg. In others it was the smell of urine or perfume. Most had that dry, stifling air of an old place closed up, embalmed for winter. But mostly it was the lack of payment that was getting to Peter. He felt he was failing Costa's trust in him. Since he had been named general manager, the rent receipts had fallen off by more than half. There was not enough to even justify his salary or make mortgage payments on all the buildings. Costa had told him it was because of the new welfare payment law, and that it wasn't his fault. Still, there was that gnawing feeling of failure that he couldn't shake. When he came to his own building, the guilt redoubled within him. Costa had saved the building and his business, and now it was paying well enough to get by. Yet there was the irony: Costa was losing out because he had opened his doors wide, and Peter was succeeding because he had done all the wrong things. He had excluded the welfare types entirely. Peter's head was throbbing as the morning progressed, and only the occasional thought of meeting Sheila for lunch kept him from calling off the rounds and going home.

At noon Peter stood in front of the Detroit Art Museum waiting for Sheila. He stood next to a free-form metal sculpture that, in addition to its grand imagery, was an excellent wind-breaker on a late December day. He probably should have had her meet him inside, he thought, but it

114

was just as well. The sharp, cold air was cleaning his senses. It was clean air, odorless, with only the noise of its own motion to carry it along. Peter was drinking in the air when he felt a chilled index finger touch him on the back of the neck. Peter turned to look down at Sheila. She was bundled up in her heavy wool coat, a skating cap, and a wool scarf wrapped around her head like a bandit's mask. Only her nose and cheeks, both wind-reddened, and her brown eyes were in sight. "Are you warm enough?" Peter chided as he took the bundle of clothes and girl in his arms. She buried her face in his coat front, and they held there for a long minute. Then she broke away from him and ran up the steps into the museum. Peter followed in a run. Inside they hugged and laughed, and elicited a frown from the guard at the door. Peter felt good now, and the scowling gray-headed guard only made him smile in a way that both recognized and made light of the authority.

Peter automatically led Sheila toward the medieval section of the many-corridored building. It was his favorite place, and whenever he needed time alone, he would come here. His room was a seventeenth-century chapel, "brought from Canterbury, England, and reassembled, courtesy of . . ." the sign said. It was a small chapel, of dark oak beams that vaulted up to the ceiling. The ceiling was of large block stones that Peter felt must have been part of the original monastery. This was his quiet place, and now he was sharing it with Sheila.

"Christ, it's beautiful," Sheila said. She seemed drawn to a stone crucifix that dominated one wall.

"And people hardly come into this room," Peter said. "I guess it's not on the main museum route. It makes me feel calm inside," Sheila said. She came over to Peter and leaned up against him.

"Yeah, I guess that's what it does for me, too. Sheila, I wanted you to meet me here in my room. I want to ask you something important."

"Don't, Peter, I don't want to talk serious right now. Let's not spoil things."

"Sheila, I think we're good for each other, and . . . ."

"No, Peter, not yet. You don't know me yet. There's too much I haven't told you." She sat down on a stone bench with lion's paws for legs and looked away from Peter. Let's not spoil things by talking about marriage or your mother or anything like that. Not now, anyways."

115

Just then an older couple entered the chapel and began touching the walls. "Can't believe people actually lived in drafty old castles," the man said. "Creepy, ain't it?" his wife responded.

Peter and Sheila looked at each other and giggled. Then Peter extended his hand to her, and they went downstairs by way of the circular stairwell, also medieval, and went into the courtyard. The courtyard was a cafeteria, surrounded by what appeared to be castle walls. The glass-domed roof, three stories up, and the plants decorating the edges gave the impression of a sidewalk café in summer. Peter felt a gentleness about his courtyard, too, though it was belied by the clanking dishes, the S. S. Kresge sign over the sandwich counter and the hordes of chattering tourists. They ate at a corner table, saying little to one another with words. There was something about this woman that didn't demand he entertain, that he talk to fill a void. He was himself with her, no hustles, no wordplay.

Peter had to get back to the rounds, but he lingered with Sheila. He drew out the meal and took the long way through the museum's corridors back to the front door. He bundled her up, wrapping the long scarf around her face as he had first seen it.

"I feel like playing hooky from those buildings," he said.

"No, you can't. We both have things to do. Oh, that reminds me. Your boss called the building."

"Costa?"

"Yes. I wrote his message down somewheres." She removed a glove and rifled through her purse. "Here it is. He says to meet him at the John R. building at four o'clock. He wants to show the building to some men, but I didn't get their names."

"Hey, Peter," a heavy voice said from the doorway. He knew it instantly as his Uncle Bert's. He looked to see Bert, in his police sergeant's uniform brushing snow off his coat. "I've been looking for you all over. Saw your old VW outside and figured you'd be in here."

Peter felt intruded on. Bert didn't belong here, he thought. "Hi, Bert," Peter said. "This is a friend of mine, Sheila Meade. Sheila, this is my Uncle Bert."

Bert was an imposing man, six feet and squared off. He looked bearlike in his long coat and plastic bagged hat. Peter watched their expressions closely. Sheila seemed to shrink in his presence. Bert peered down at her with no more emotion than if he were writing her a ticket for jaywalking.

"Yes, ma'am," Bert said. "I've heard all about you from Peter's mother. Say, would you mind if I talked to Peter alone for a minute? I'm on duty, and I got to be back out in a minute or my partner will raise hell."

"There's nothing you can't say in front of Sheila," Peter said.

"That's OK," Sheila said, "I've really got to go now. I'll see you later on, Peter." Peter watched Sheila push out the heavy outer door and disappear.

"What's this about, Bert?"

"What do you know about that girl, Pug?"

"Don't call me Pug," Peter said. "That was the nickname his father had always used, and he didn't like the sound of it coming from Bert. "And don't say anything about Sheila. I know everything I need to know about her."

Bert took off his hat and banged it against a pillar to shake off the melted snow. Peter couldn't help but be startled by the physical resemblance to his dead father. "You know everything you need to know, or everything you want to know?"

"It's the same thing."

"Oh, then you know that she's been busted four times for prostitution."

Peter couldn't answer. He couldn't say anything at all.

"You know she dances at the Tender Trap, bottomless and topless. And I guess she's even told you her ex-husband is a big black stud named Giles Meade. He's serving a ten-year stint in Jackson Prison for manslaughter."

"I don't believe you. Mother put you up to this."

"Look here, Peter. Your mother's concerned that you are making serious noises about this girl. She asked me to see if you weren't getting yourself into a mess. You ought to know I don't like putting anyone down, but I have an obligation to your father."

Peter walked over to the door and leaned his head against the pane of glass. It felt cool against his skin.

117

"Alls I'm saying is this isn't the girl to take home to Mom," Bert said. He put a hand on his shoulder. "Your daddy and I had some wild times ourselves. By God, we probably have more than one snot-nosed little bastard running around this town 'cause of him and me. But you don't buy a cow when everone's milking it for free."

Peter jerked his shoulder away from Bert. "You . . . you tell Mom she did it fine this time. You tell her I'm moving out. I'll send up for my things. You thank her for snooping into Sheila's life. Don't forget, Bert, thank her."

"I won't tell her no such thing. It's not her fault you picked up a whore."

Peter grabbed Bert by the coat and pushed him up against a pillar. "Get out of here, you goddamned pig. Get out."

Peter went back up the museum stairs to his secluded chapel. He sat on the gray-stone bench Sheila had so recently occupied. He looked up at the stone crucifix, and he wept.


Chuck sat in his car in front of the John R. building. He half listened to the news report on the radio and glanced frequently at his watch. It was four-twenty. The Goldsmiths were late. Peter was late. He lit a Chesterfield and listened to the announcer recounting the latest Detroit homicide. "Number 789 this year," he said. Police Chief Spreen was quoted as estimating that the murder toll would top 800 in the two weeks left in the year. "The highest murder rate per capita of any American city," the announcer said. Chuck hoped as he listened that the Goldsmiths didn't have the radio turned on in their car, or that would be enough to turn them back to the suburbs.

Peter Balantine got in the car on the passenger's side. Chuck looked at him, but Peter was looking forward over the hood.

"Where did you come from? I didn't see any car," Chuck asked.

"I walked from the museum. It's only a couple of blocks from here," Peter said.

Chuck could read the obvious. Something was wrong with Peter. "Rent receipts any better today?" Peter shook his head no.

"Then what's eating you? You look like you just lost your best friend."

118

"What do you know about Sheila Meade?" Peter asked. He kept his head down, his arms folded against his chest.

"So, that's it."

"What do you know?"

"I knew her mother. She was one of the tenants in my first building. Now there was a woman that could complain."

"Did you know," Peter stopped and paused for a long minute, "did you know Sheila is a prostitute?"

"I don't think that's right. Where did you get it?"

"She's got a record for prostitution."

"When?" Chuck said. He looked at his watch again. It was four-thirty.

"Who cares when?"

"Maybe you should. There aren't too many kids in this neighborhood who haven't tried to break out the fast way. The guys steal cars, roll drunks; the girls turn a few tricks. You can't blame them. They see the whole damn world on the tube, then they flick it off and look at poverty. In Malta we were poor and didn't know it. Here people keep reminding you of it."

"Not prostitution."

"Get off it, Peter. You pitying yourself, or her? Girls out in the suburbs can give it away, but a kid down here turns a trick to buy a dress or some groceries, and she's a hooker. The important thing is now. Is she still peddling? Lot's of kids go through a stage. The better ones come out of it."

"I can't buy that."

"Who's asking you to? You want to be a moralist, fine. That's no business of mine. But don't come down on everyone with that holier-than-thou attitude. I don't want to hear it."

A black Cadillac pulled up behind Chuck's Eldorado. He could see the Goldsmith brothers sitting like bookends on opposite sides of the front seat. "The Goldsmiths are here. We got to sell them on this building, so don't say anything negative about anything or anyone. That pair will turn and run if you start to pucker up to say 'boo.'"

Chuck went out and opened the door for one of the Goldsmiths. Both came out. "You're going to love this building," Chuck said. "I've got a building manager here who's a beaut. She keeps the place up and the

119

troublemakers out. Now take a look at the brick in this building, common brick. You know how much you'd have to pay to build an apartment complex like this today?'' Chuck went on with his sales spiel, moving the Goldsmiths one step at a time into the building. He talked about the furnace, about the good tenants, about the plumbing, and he moved them into the lobby. As he entered, Chuck heard a wailing sound, a crying so loud that even the radio music from the rooms was muted.

"What's that sound?" a Goldsmith brother asked.

"I don't hear anything, do you Peter? It's probably a television set going. Now take a look at this woodwork. That's white oak, impossible to buy anywhere today." Chuck kept talking, and motioned to Peter to find out who was screaming upstairs while he practiced diversionary tactics with the Goldsmiths. Peter left, but the wailing sound didn't stop. Finally Chuck couldn't hold them off any longer. He led them upstairs.

There she was. Mrs. Brown spread out in the hallway, a mountain of flesh, most of it exposed. She was crying, sobbing, and screaming at a near-panic pitch. Peter was trying to get her to her feet, without success. "Leaves me alone," she yelled. "Oh my goodness, leaves me be. He left me. Ooooh, he left me." As Chuck neared, he got a good whiff of her. She stunk with a smell that was at once redolent of stale beer and body odor. "Oooh, Lordy, he's left me," she continued to wail.

The Goldsmiths plastered themselves against the wall and stared at the incredible sight. "What's that?" one of them whispered to Chuck.

"Well, ah, she's my building manager," Chuck said.

Out of the corner of his eye Chuck noticed Martin Luther peering out around the partially open apartment door. He walked over to Mrs. Brown and pulled her skirt down over her thighs.

Peter was still trying to move her by pulling on an arm. "Mrs. Brown," Peter said as he tugged, "you're fired. You hear me, Mrs. Brown? You're fired."

"Oh, my Lord, he's done left me. Ooooh."

"No use, Peter. We can't move a mountain, not even to sell this place. Gentlemen," Chuck said. He couldn't help smiling at the Goldsmiths' bewildered expressions. "I assume you'd like me to escort you back to your car."

120

# 9

"Tomorrow is Christmas Eve," Chuck said into the telephone receiver. "You want to cut off electricity to five thousand people on Christmas Eve, be my guest. I can see the headlines now: 'Detroit Edison turns off five thousand Christmas Trees on Welfare Children.' "

It was a cheap trick, and Chuck knew it, but it bought him a few days of grace on the electric bill. He couldn't pay the bill, no way, not even a good faith payment. But he knew the electric company didn't have the nerve to unplug his people. It would buy time—not much, but enough, he felt, to come up with a solution.

Chuck hung up the phone and tossed the note from the electric company in the center of the disheveled pile of papers, notes, and unopened mail on his desk. There was no order to things since Marilyn had left, and no money to hire another secretary. Anita had tried to help out when she wasn't minding the children, but she wasn't a part of the operation and couldn't decipher the scribbled matchbook covers and clipped messages that Chuck was accustomed to. The office was in disarray. The newspapers were stacked in a pile next to his desk. There was no need to read them. Cluttering the room were the cardboard boxes filled to overflowing with clothing, toys, and canned goods. They were the boxes that Chuck would give out tomorrow on Christmas Eve. There

121

weren't as many boxes this year because Chuck hadn't had as much time to pester merchants for handouts and had no more credit to buy on his own accounts. Maybe he could find time today to hit a couple more businessmen, he thought. No, he had a business to run. Jimmy had been complaining that dope addicts were moving in on his building. The Brush Street building was having heating problems. Four buildings had had their mailboxes ripped off the day before, losing some more of the welfare checks that were addressed to tenants. Whenever a mailbox was torn off, a city inspector was close behind, issuing the landlord a violation. Violations were stacking up, too, each one carrying $250 to $500 fines or ninety days in jail. Chuck brushed them aside to think about getting some working capital, but ended thinking about finding the family a place in the suburbs. He could hear his dog in the basement. Buster was barking out his prejudices at the scent of some children passing by outside. Chuck's thoughts that morning were as disheveled as his office.

The phone rang. It was Ralph O'Hara. "The creditors have been getting after me, Chuck. I think it's time to talk about legal remedy."

"What, no I-told-you-so's?"

"I wouldn't say that, Chuck. Honest, I wouldn't say that at all. It's no shame to dissolve a business."

"Bankruptcy," Chuck said. "Call it by its name. And I'm not ready for it yet. I've got some other sources, some friends who'll back me. You tell those vultures Chuck Costa is good for it."

"Be reasonable, Chuck. There's no hope of catching back up. You owe the gas company alone twelve thousand dollars."

"No sweat. I'll come up with it. You heard whether the police caught up with my little blond bomber yet?"

"Susan Stanicki? She's disappeared since we filed the formal complaint. Police think she's still in the area, but so far they haven't caught her. What we need is a Columbo on the case."

Things must be bad, Chuck thought, for Ralph to start coming up with one-liners to break tension. "Problem with those TV detectives," Chuck said, "is they always end the show after they've arrested the bad guys and just before the judge lets them off."

"Always making with the jokes."

"Why not? I can't seem to make anything else. Say Ralph, can we get some of that money out of those bonds you talked me into last year? You know, the ones for the kids?"

"That's only a few hundred dollars, Chuck. It won't help."

"I've got to pay my people and hire a few more. Drugs are moving in on one of my buildings, and I can't afford a crew to flood them out. And there's the repairs. A few hundred would do it."

"It would take a couple of weeks to cash them in."

"The people I hire deal in cash. I guess the flooding and repairs will wait. They'll have to wait until you can cash in those bonds. Unless . . . never mind, Ralph. I just thought of a moneylender I can hit up. I'll call you tomorrow."

Chuck hung up and went directly to his car. He knew what he had to do now, and he knew if he waited to think about it, he wouldn't do it. He drove down Woodward Avenue into the heart of the shopping district. The sidewalks were overflowing with crowds of people, bundled to the hilt, laden with last-minute Christmas purchases. The street poles were all decorated with plastic Santas and candy canes. Outside speakers were blaring out carols and jingles, and the Salvation Army Santas were ringing their bells and leaning on their red kettles. At another time Chuck might have slowed down to take in the setting, to let Christmas overtake him, but not now. He turned onto Monroe Street.

Chuck parked his car in the long shadow of the twin towers of Saint Mary's Cathedral on Saint Antoine Street and walked into Greektown. The names on the signs spoke of Athenian proprietors: Peloponnesos, Stemma, and Ambrosia. The tourist council called it Detroit's purely Greek enclave, but Chuck was well aware that a part of its innards was Sicilian. Here, while the farmer's wife from Wapakoneta sampled shish kebab, and baklava out front, an ethnic pageant of quite another sort was going on in one back office. Lieutenants, like personifications of vices on a medieval stage—drug men, juice men, pimps, gamblers, and hit men—all would pass in review as Antonio Genotti held mafioso court. And all just one short block from Detroit Police Headquarters.

Chuck slowed down as he walked this street. He stopped at the Delphi Bakery window and browsed through the display. He was reluctant to continue down the block to Sparta Restaurant, to enter and ask Antonio for a juice loan. Chuck was well aware of the rates from a loan shark: ten percent per week on the original note and no late payments. He had known one man in one of his buildings who had fallen behind in his payments for four weeks. The man now is missing four fingers on his right hand. Chuck hesitated. A horn blew, and he looked to the street. There was a long black limousine standing at the curb. Antonio Genotti was in the back seat waving at Chuck. He walked over to the car.

*"Ciao, Costa, come sta il mio amico maltese?"* Genotti said. He opened the door wide and motioned for Chuck to get into the back with him. Chuck obeyed.

*"Come sta la sua famiglia?"* Chuck asked.

*"Bene.* My girl is graduating this year from Albion College. And little Toni is off to law school."

"Things are well with you, Antonio."

"But not with you, hey, Costa? I hear you're having some dough shortages. Were you coming to see me about it?"

"Perhaps."

"So, Chucky Costa is coming to me, the man who didn't want me to buy in three years ago. It was three years ago, wasn't it, Chucky? You didn't want my people in your buildings then."

"It was nothing personal, Antonio. I wanted to keep them legitimate."

"How much you need, Chucky? Five C's, ten C's?" Antonio crossed his legs, and Chuck noticed his shoes, alligator shoes with the bottoms as impeccably polished as the tops.

"If that was all I needed, I would have gone to one of your boys, Antonio. I need fifty thousand dollars to keep my buildings going. I'll sell you quarter interest in the business for that."

Antonio reached forward and tapped the black driver on the shoulder, motioning him to drive the car around. He reached inside of his plaid jacket and pulled out a package of cigarettes, a menthol brand. He pulled a large white plastic cigarette holder out of another pocket and jointed the cigarette with the holder. "This is a charcoal filter to strain nicotine," Antonio said. "It's like sucking air through a screen door, but my doctor says I got to give up smoking. You smoke, don't you Chucky?"

124

"Yes, Antonio."

"Not good. You don't care about your health."

"Nobody lives forever. Now, about the money. I'm offering you a straight business deal. Twenty-five percent of all of my receipts."

"Chucky, I got ears. I know you are about to go under. Why should I pay for a piece of your headaches?"

"It can be a good business again."

Antonio drew hard on the cigarette. "Hell," he said and tossed the cigarette and holder into the ashtray. He leaned forward and tapped the driver on the shoulder. "Tobacco," he said, and the driver handed back three black cigars. Antonio lit one. "Tell you what, Chucky. I'll give you the loan for fifty-one percent, but you got to open up your buildings to my people. Your managers could make a little extra running numbers for me."

"And pushers?"

"It's all part of the business."

Chuck sat back in the leather seat. It gave evenly around his back. "I've got to have some time to think on that deal, Antonio."

"Sure, Chucky. I don't muscle people to get in, but if you come in, we got to do business."

The limousine pulled up in front of the bakery where Chuck had been picked up. "Let me sleep on it, Antonio. I'll call you sometime tomorrow." Chuck got out of the car and started to walk away.

"Hey, Chuck," Antonio yelled after him. Chuck looked and saw an arm extended out from the limousine window. The hand had a diamond on it as large as an ice cube, and in the hand were two black cigars. Chuck went back to the car and leaned over to hear what Antonio had to say. He slipped the two cigars into Chuck's vest pocket. "You're right, Chucky, nobody does live forever. Merry Christmas, hey?"

"Yeah, Antonio, Merry Christmas."

Chuck was shivering as he got in his car and drove away from Greektown. The car heater was pumping out warmth, but Chuck couldn't feel it. The thought of bringing in Mafia money scared him. He would face off a bunch of street hoods, whose memories were as short as their tempers, but the Cosa Nostra lacked temper and never lost out on a debt. It was the code of *omertà*, the "noble silence," that meant "be quiet or die." As a boy in Malta Chuck had heard all the old tales about

125

how *omertà* was always enforced on every continent, anywhere in the world. Malta was only fifty miles from Sicily; surnames were identical in both countries, yet the Maltese had avoided falling under mafiosi control.

In Malta there had at once been a respect for mafiosi history and an abhorrence for its influence. Every Maltese schoolboy knew of how the secret society arose as resistance to French Angevin conquerors. The mafiosi brought hope to the occupied island, carried food to the poor, and dealt vengeance to the Bourbon tyrants. The Maltese, having been under occupational governments of many countries, understood the Sicilian mafiosi's story. But the story didn't end when Italy was again unified. The mafiosi, having no foreign throats to cut, turned on its own. It was a cure worse than the cause. Chuck wondered if bringing Mafia money into his business would not end the same. When he had thought to go to Antonio, it was with the understanding that much syndicate money goes into legitimate business. Food produce, garment manufacturing, vending machines, labor unions, bars, restaurants, were all honest businesses backed by underworld money. Chuck had hoped Antonio would see his housing business as an honest money investment, but Antonio had other ideas. He wanted to use the buildings. Why not? Chuck thought, they've been working around my buildings right along. What was the difference if now they would be inside looking out? Chuck really didn't believe these thoughts, but how many alternatives did he have? The thought of returning to peddling eggs from the trunk of his car because some bleeding hearts in the state capitol changed a law infuriated him; the thought of resorting to the syndicate still frightened him. He was, as he had heard many of his Appalachian tenants say, between the rock and the hard place.

Chuck drove around to think. His car seemed to gravitate automatically toward the streets where he owned buildings. He drove past them, thinking of the people within them, the good ones more than the bad. He had no idea where they would go if he had to close down, nor what would happen to them if he let organized crime move in. He was driving down Twelfth Street, his thoughts still in Greektown, when he saw the crowd in front of his building. Chuck pulled over and pushed his way into the lobby.

Peter and three tenants were crowded next to the stairs. Chuck

126

pushed in and saw Jimmy lying sideways on the steps, his face smashed open, his blood flowing onto the runner. Chuck bent down close to Jimmy's face.

"What happened?" Chuck asked. Jimmy didn't answer. His eyes were closed.

"I got here first," Peter said. "Jimmy was still conscious. He said a guy told him there was a fire up on four. He ran up the stairs, and they caught him, two men coming down and another coming up behind him. Jimmy said it was over in a minute."

Chuck heard the ambulance pull up outside. He began to pick Jimmy up.

"Don't move him," Peter said. "Let the attendants do it." The two men came in with a stretcher, and within minutes the lobby was empty except for Chuck and Peter. Chuck leaned his back against a wall and lit a Chesterfield. "Did he say who did it?"

"He didn't have to. In two weeks this building has turned into a dope den. The fourth floor is alive with addicts. You can bet one of them had a hand in it."

Chuck went into Jimmy's apartment and straight to the kitchen where he knew Jimmy kept his gun. He noticed a pile of unopened mail on the counter. Who'd write to Jimmy, he thought, then pushed the mail aside and opened the cabinet. The gun was on the hook. Chuck pulled it off and checked the chambers. It was loaded. He slipped it into his belt.

"What are you doing?" Peter asked.

"What I should have done last week. I'm going to flood the building, right now."

Peter stood in front of the kitchen door. "Don't be crazy. You can't clean them out without some backup men."

"Get out of my way, kid. I've got a job to do." Chuck was getting madder by the second. He was trying not to let it out on Peter.

"You told me yourself you can't go after them when you're heated up. You'll be reacting on their level."

Chuck realized that Peter was right. He had learned his lessons well, and now he was parroting them back. "OK, we'll run them off next week. Now let's get to the hospital and see if we have a building manager here."

Neither man spoke for several minutes as they drove up Cass

Avenue. Finally Chuck cut the silence. "Georgie tells me you moved into the John R. building."

"Yes, I figured we needed a manager in the building now that Mrs. Brown isn't doing it."

"She still drinking?"

"No, but she's still whining. She's apologized to me several times and says she can handle the building again if we give her a chance."

"You think we should?" Chuck asked. He thought Peter looked surprised by the question.

"Of course not. She had her chance and made a fool of you."

"That's been done before. But we need managers, and before her boyfriend dumped her, she was a good one."

"She had her chance."

Chuck smiled. "You're the general manager; I'll let you use your own judgment on it."

"But you wouldn't do it that way?"

"No, I guess I wouldn't."

"Look, Chuck. I haven't been doing a very good job of collecting rents, and maybe you should get—"

"You agreed to the job, remember? You wanted to be a landlord. I think you'd better stick it out. I couldn't do any better as it is. And I don't have the time to. Sounds to me like you're gonna whine a little yourself."

"What's that supposed to mean?" Peter asked.

"How's Sheila, if it's any of my business?"

"It isn't. I haven't seen her."

"Your hard line scares me a little, Peter. You gotta give people more room," Chuck said. He slowed to fifteen miles an hour as he entered the Wayne State University traffic area.

"That sounds funny coming from you, Chuck."

Chuck slammed on the brakes and nearly tossed Peter into the windshield. "There she is," he said, "over there by the Old Main Building."

"Who?"

"Susan Stanicki, our bomber." Chuck stared to make sure. His car resting in the traffic midstream stopped all movement and inspired a

128

cacophony of horns. The noise drew the girl's attention. She stopped at the building entrance and looked directly at Chuck's car. It was her, he was certain. He thought she seemed just as certain of recognizing him, for she turned and ran into the building. A bearded young man Chuck hadn't noticed standing near her ran into the building after her. Chuck jumped out of the car and went after her.

As he climbed the stone steps leading to the entrance, Chuck realized it was futile to try and catch someone in the Old Main Building. The hundred-year-old structure hid an architectural hodgepodge behind its ivy-hung towers. Annexes had been spliced onto annexes, staircases led in every direction, yet many of them ended in dead ends. On one floor alone, he recalled, the only way to get from Room 218 to Room 219 was to go downstairs and up a different staircase again. Yet he felt the rage coming up within him, and he knew he had to try and catch her. He entered.

The hall was alive with bodies in motion, with heads bobbing in and out of doorways and flowing down the hallway like corks in a swift current. Above the heads Chuck saw her in the elevator. The door closed. He elbowed his way up the nearest flight of stairs to the second floor. He went into each classroom and looked around. Students were entering, mingling, taking seats. The bell rang. They looked at him as if he were a bag of garbage someone had dropped in the way. He didn't belong there, but no one seemed anxious to volunteer to remove him.

At the next-to-the-last door on the second floor he saw her inside, sitting in the far row, still with the bearded youth alongside her. He entered and went straight for her.

"May I help you?" Chuck heard the instructor ask, but he paid no attention as he crossed the room filled with obstacles. The girl jumped up and made it out the room's back door. When Chuck got to the door, her male companion was standing in front of it, looking down at Chuck and waving his hands as if to shoo him off. Chuck hit him only once in the stomach; it was enough to double him over and push him out of the way.

The hall was silent, no students, and no Susan Stanicki. Chuck had no idea which way she could have gone. He saw an exit sign at the end of the hall and thought how appealing that word might have looked to her.

Chuck opened the door and stepped out onto a metal grid fire escape. He looked down into the alley. There was his car. Peter was standing in front of it holding Stanicki at arm's length as she tried to kick him.

"This what you were looking for?" Peter asked. He grinned up at Chuck.

"It sure is." Chuck was down to the ground in half a minute. "How did you know where she'd come out?"

"You forget I was a Wayne student myself once."

"No, I didn't forget; I overlooked it," Chuck said. "Now, Miss Stanicki, you mind telling me why you stoned my office and blew up my building?"

Susan was livid with rage. She was squirming. "You bastards had it coming. The way you take advantage of the poor. You deserved it, all of you!"

"Get in the back seat and sit on her," Chuck said. "I'm going to take her for a ride." Peter looked puzzled, but he did what Chuck said. Five minutes later they were stopped in front of the bombed-out building. Chuck stopped for only a minute. "Did you teach me a lesson with that, Miss Stanicki?" She didn't answer. "Let me show you what you accomplished." He drove another block and stopped in front of another building.

"You're going inside with me, and if you don't act civil, I'm going to treat you as I would a man who messed me up. Women's lib, all the way."

"This is kidnapping," she said.

Chuck got out and pulled her out by the arm. He squeezed tight to let her know he was serious. "It might be murder if you don't shut up." Chuck pushed Susan ahead up the stairs to the third floor. Peter followed. He knocked on Apartment 3B. A small Mexican woman with wiry hair answered.

"*Buenos días*, Mrs. Rodriguez," Chuck said. "I thought I'd stop in and see how you and the kids are doing since the fire."

"*Gracias, entre, por favor.*" It was a small apartment with what appeared to be wall-to-wall children. Chuck knew there were eight children in all, but the way they were moving around the place, they seemed to be an army.

"Mrs. Rodriguez lost everything she had in the firebombing, Susan. All of the children's clothing, all of their Christmas presents, and the few sticks of furniture they owned."

"You have been most generous with the clothing and things, Mr. Costa." She looked at Susan. "He had that tree sent over for the children." The woman pointed to a small tree near the window, decorated with paper cutouts and about a dozen bulbs. It was a pathetic tree, and Susan turned her face away from it.

"You have Susan to thank for the tree, Mrs. Rodriguez," Chuck said. The woman beamed with appreciation. "You see, Susan here was the one responsible for bombing the other building."

Mrs. Rodriguez's expression changed to one of surprise. "You are kidding, no?"

"No. She said she did it because she wanted to help the poor. I'm taking her to the police, but I wanted you to meet her first."

Mrs. Rodriguez came close to Susan. Chuck held her arm and could feel her body going limp under Mrs. Rodriguez's stare. "Why you do this to me?" the woman said. Not viciously, but with a genuine pleading in her voice. "My children did not hurt you. Why did you want to burn up their toys?" Susan's face was turned away. Mrs. Rodriguez reached up with a dark, leathery hand and turned Susan's face toward her own. "She is a child, Mr. Costa. She could not do such a thing."

"Please, let me out of here," Susan yelled. "I've got to get out of here."

Chuck took her back down to the car and put her in the back seat. Peter and Chuck got in and drove her to the police station. She said nothing during the trip or, later, to the officer at the desk. They booked her, and Chuck and Peter continued on to the hospital.

In the emergency room the same redheaded woman was at the desk. "Excuse me," Chuck said.

"Yes? Why, it's Mr. Costa, isn't it? You're becoming one of our best customers."

"Thank you. I always try to patronize the better businesses. Now, can you tell me what condition Jimmy Caldwell is in?"

The nurse looked on the chart and smiled. "He's unconscious."

"Serious?" Peter asked.

"No, drunk. He has a broken jaw, numerous stitches, and four fractured ribs, but, according to the chart, he wasn't feeling any pain when they brought him in."

Chuck couldn't help but laugh. "That's Jimmy. We'll be back after he dries out. See you next year."

# 10

Everyone was acting up in class on the next to the last day of school
before Christmas vacation. It was expected, and the teachers were
fortunate if they could maintain order, let alone teach. Pam Costa was no
exception for a seventh grader on this day. She whispered to her girl
friends on either side, passed notes, talked in study hall, and generally
let the spirit of the occasion reach her. Last period was art, a free-for-all
under normal circumstances, chaos today. Pam was more serious this
hour, for she had a task to complete. The second ashtray she was making
for her father for Christmas still had to have its last coat of glaze, then a
final visit to the kiln. Pam had gotten behind in the week-long project,
trying to shape the clay into a circle, a feat never quite accomplished,
and the hand painting took more time than it might have. But she wanted
to make two ashtrays, one for Dad's office and one for home. If she was
to complete the second, today was it. The ashtray had to be left overnight
to be ready for vacation tomorrow. She finished her glazing, then got in
line to use the kiln. Only six items could go in at once, but Pam was sixth
in line, so she knew she would make it in time.

Two girls near the front of the line let Janice McCoy take cuts. Pam
was furious. As number seven she couldn't get her ashtray finished.
Normally Pam would have been afraid of speaking up against Janice

McCoy. The girl was big, hoody, and had a clique of Appalachian buddies that were to a girl all bigger than Pam. But she was mad, Christmas depended on it, and she spoke out. "Mrs. Catalpa," Pam said, "Janice took cuts in line."

The art teacher, a willowy black woman Pam had always felt at ease with, came over. "Is that true, Janice?"

"My friends saved me this spot," she said. The girls on either side nodded a vigorous agreement.

"You can't save places, Janice. You'll have to go to the back of the line."

"Bullshit," Janice said. She stepped out of line and threw her ashtray on a work table, so hard that it broke in two. "See what you done?" she said to Pam. "You're a squealer."

"That's enough, Janice," Mrs. Catalpa said. She came over and placed a firm hand on her shoulder. Janice pulled away. "All right, young lady, you may spend the rest of the period in the detention hall."

The incident, however, was not closed. After class next day Pam took her books from her locker, and, carrying her finished ashtray on top of them, went down the back stairwell. Janice and three of her friends encircled Pam by the door. Janice took the ashtray away from Pam and broke it in half on a fire extinguisher.

"Give that back," Pam said, and reached for it. All the girls jumped on Pam at once. She struggled, but it was useless. They had her pinned down on the dirty cement floor. Janice took out a pair of scissors and waved them in front of Pam's face. "You ain't gonna be teacher's pet anymore," she said. She began cutting Pam's hair. With each sound of the snip, Pam could see her long brown hair being pulled away. She struggled viciously, contorted her body, and kicked. Pam broke the hold of one of the girls and, with her free hand, gouged the other in the face with her fingernails. Someone was coming. The girls ran. Pam was left sitting on the floor, holding half of her ashtray and staring in disbelief at her hair scattered around her on the floor.


Chuck's office was in a festive mood that morning. It was Christmas Eve day, a day when tenants came around for the baskets of clothing, toys, and canned foods that Chuck had amassed. It was a tradition that Chuck had maintained ever since he saw his business taking hold five years earlier. Chuck and Peter used the time between callers to go over the books. They came in by ones and twos, women mostly, and accepted the baskets with, if not thanks, at least a gesture of friendship. At one point Peter was about to chastise a tenant who came for a basket, yet hadn't paid her rent in a month. Chuck stopped him. It was Christmas, and Chuck wanted at least this two-day holiday to come off without a hassle.

Around two P.M. he had a couple of callers who were not expected. One was Mrs. Geraldine Forsythe, a suburban landlady whom Chuck knew only vaguely. She was a matronly woman of about fifty and would have passed for plain if it were not for the full-length mink coat that engulfed her and the display of diamond rings on her hands. Mr. Forsythe came in behind her, carrying a large basket of toys.

"I heard how you give out presents to the poor people, Mr. Costa," she said. She sat down with her coat still wrapped around her. "I thought it was such a kind gesture that I ought to do my share. My husband gathered up used toys from children all over the neighborhood, and since I knew the area, I was nominated to bring them down."

"That's very nice of you," Chuck said.

"Yes, well, I had a building down here last year, and my husband and I did the same thing then. Only it was such a violent building that I had to have my husband go in and send the children out to the car to get the presents."

"Oh," Chuck said.

"Oh, yes, they were such darling children, really. It was such fun to see them taking the toys."

"You won't see any children here, Mrs. Forsythe."

"Really?"

"No, I have a rule about giving. The parents come and get the presents." Chuck got up from his desk and walked around front to talk to this woman. She irritated him immensely, and he wanted her to know it. "You see, you don't do anyone favors by tossing them crumbs. They'll only hate your guts for it."

Mrs. Forsythe fidgeted at the word "guts." "Oh, really?" she said.

135

"I don't want that, Mrs. Forsythe, and I don't want to pat their curly heads and have them look up to me. A child needs parents to look up to. The mamma or, even better, the daddy should come in with the presents. He's the one they need to admire. Not me."

Mrs. Forsythe got up and began backing out the door. "Yes, that does make sense. I guess I never thought of it in those terms."

Anita entered by the side hall door. Chuck read her expression and went to meet her. She told him about Pam, how the school nurse had brought her home in near hysteria. She told him about the hair and the fight. Chuck excused himself and went directly up to Pam's room.

From the door he could hear her sobbing. "Can I come in, honey?" he asked, then entered without waiting for a reply. Pam lay across the bed, her face in a pillow, her hair hanging over one shoulder. Chuck saw the wide gaps where hair had been cut out, in some spots cut up to within an inch of her scalp. He sat on the edge of the bed and rubbed her back for several minutes. She went on sobbing.

"Pam, Mom will take you to the beauty shop this afternoon to get a fancy new hairdo—a rinse, set, the works. Honey, they can fix your hair so it will look fine, just fine," Chuck said. But as he looked at the swatches of hair, he wondered if it could be made consistent with anything less than a brush cut.

"Can you keep a secret?" Chuck asked. Pam looked up from the pillow and stopped crying. "I've found us a new home in Farmington. It's a nice place, honey. The kids are all good kids."

"Will I have to go back to school, here?"

"Not even once. We'll move out there next week, and when school starts after vacation, you'll be in a good school."

"Oh, Daddy," she said, and buried her head in his chest and cried.

"It's a nice house, too," Chuck said. He thought of the place he had looked at last week. A rent with an option to buy. He hadn't been able to decide on it. Now he had no choice. "It's not as big as this house. There's no basement or upstairs, but it's got a yard big enough to keep horses. Buster can run free. But don't tell your mother, we'll take her out there tomorrow and surprise her. Promise?"

Pam reached up and felt her hair. "Oh, Daddy, I can't go to a new school like this."

"I told you, your mother will take you to the beauty shop today. Why, I'll even toss a new school dress into the deal. Don't worry, Pam, you'll be beautiful." Chuck got up and went to the door.

"Daddy," Pam said. She reached over the bed and picked up the two pieces of her ashtray. "I made this for you, but they broke it." She began to cloud up again.

"Thanks, honey. I can fix it like new. It's beautiful." He set the ashtray aside and picked Pam up in a hug as he used to do when she was the baby. "We'll fix everything. Don't worry."

Chuck went down to the kitchen. Anita was standing at the sink with her back to him. Chuck went over and put on the tea kettle, then sat down. Anita turned around; tears were running down her cheeks.

"Pam's going to be fine, 'Nit. There's nothing to cry about."

"You got a phone call while you were upstairs," Anita said. "It was from Antonio Genotti's secretary saying he will be in church all afternoon, and left a number where he could be reached."

Chuck came over to the sink and took the slip of paper from her hand and placed it in his pants pocket.

"Chuck, you can't get involved with the Mafia. You can't do it."

"Anita, I run my own business. Don't tell me what to do."

"All that talk about your tenants. How can you sell them to the Mafia? And us, what about the children?"

"We're about to go under, Anita. Can't you understand that? I've got to do something to save us."

"By selling your friends and family?"

"No. We're talking about a loan. And what would it matter if I opened up my buildings anyway? Do you really think anyone cares? They call me slumlord, don't they? They throw rocks at my house, butcher my children. They're animals, Anita. You were right when you said they hate us. They hate our guts, so who gives a damn about them?"

"You do, Chuck."

"Like hell I do." Buster began to bark violently. Chuck went out the door and down into the basement. He sat on the bottom step. Buster came up and licked his face. Chuck rubbed him behind the ears and looked at the scar across his nose. The flesh had healed, but the scar was still visible where the kid had cut him. Outside someone was passing.

Buster turned his head to the side and growled, low and determined. What are they doing to us, Buster? Chuck thought. What are they doing to all of us?

Upstairs Peter was sitting at Chuck's desk making a few final entries into the ledger. Mrs. Forsythe had gone, and the routine of people coming in for baskets seemed to have been shut off like a faucet. Peter was tired of the interruptions, so when the door opened and he heard someone enter, he didn't look up right away. He would finish this entry first. Peter finally brought his eyes up to face Sheila standing before him. She seemed small from behind the desk, waiflike.

"What are you doing here?" Peter asked.

"I don't know, not for sure. I guess I wanted to be sure it was over."

"I'll confirm it, it's over," Peter said. He leaned back in his chair and glared at her.

Sheila went for the door. Peter got up and ran to the door. He caught the frame with his hand as she was opening it and slammed it shut. "Look, I'm sorry. I don't mean to be cruel, but . . ."

"You're upset," she said. She looked up him with an absent expression, one he had never seen on her before, one he could not decipher.

"You lied to me about your past."

"That's not so. You never asked, or I would have told you. I wanted to. I couldn't. It would have spoiled things."

"It did."

Sheila backed away from him. "I have what I came for. Now will you let me go?"

Peter hesitated. He glanced at his hand holding the door shut, and he realized he didn't want to remove it. "I can't, Sheila. I want to, but I can't."

"Then I'll make it easy for you," she said. With both hands she tried to push him aside, but he didn't nove. Instead he grabbed her, struggled for an instant, then kissed her. Then he picked her up and set her at arm's length from himself.

"Sheila, I don't know. I want you, damned if I don't, but I don't know if I can overlook everything. Chuck calls me a moralist. I don't know about that. But I don't understand yet.''

"You can try.''

"I'd like that," Peter said. He pulled her closer to him. "But I can't make any promises. You've got to understand that.''

"None asked for," she said. Peter saw a faint, unsure smile come to her lips.

"What do you say to dinner? I'm done with the books, and I'll just tell Chuck I'm going. You wait for me in the outer office. I'll be just a minute.''

Peter went into the house and, with Anita's directions, found Chuck in the basement. He was sitting on the steps, rubbing the dog's ears. Buster growled as Peter came down.

"Anything wrong, Chuck?''

"Of course not. What's up?''

"I'd like to go now, if it's all right with you. A friend came by, and things are finished up here.''

"That friend wouldn't be Sheila, would it?''

Peter grinned. "Yes, I suppose it would be.''

"Good, I'm glad to hear it. But before you go, I've got some bad news.''

"You don't have to say it. I've seen your books.''

"I can't pay you 'til the end of January, but after that I . . . well, I don't know what then.''

"Chuck, I'd work for nothing for a while if it would help.''

"No way. You've forgotten the first rule of landlording: Pay your own way in everything.''

"No I haven't," Peter said. He slipped something into Chuck's hand.

"What's this?" Chuck asked. He squinted in the diffuse light to inspect it. A ring, silver with a diamond. "That was your dad's ring, wasn't it?''

"Yes. I want you to have it. You trained me in this business. You even saved my building. I owe you something.''

"Here," Chuck said. He held his open hand out with the ring. "I appreciate it, but this isn't just a ring.''

139

"That's why I gave it to you. Don't snub me by refusing it. We made a deal, remember? I want the deal to have two smiles to it."

"Beaten by my own words," Chuck said. He put the ring on his right hand, then extended it to Peter. "We've got a deal."

Peter left, and about fifteen minutes later Chuck came back up into the kitchen. Anita was sitting at the table crocheting something. "Come on," Chuck said to her. "I've got a couple of calls I want you in on." He pulled her to her feet and practically dragged her into the office. Chuck called Antonio Genotti and told him that he was sorry, but they couldn't make a deal. Then he called Ralph O'Hara.

"Ralph," Chuck said. "I think I'm bankrupt."

"You have been for months," Ralph said, "and didn't know it."

# 11

More than five hundred people overran the sidewalks in front of the Federal Courthouse. It was a bitter cold midwinter day, and the crowd let off enough steaming breath as they milled and huddled to make it look like a cauldron of boiling stew. The faces of the crowd were mainly black, some Spanish, some white, and a few so thoroughly unwashed as to make an estimate of complexion impossible. Some carried bundled children, others waved picket signs. "Don't Turn Off Costa," one sign read. "We'll All Be Bankrupt," read another. "We Need Mr. Costa," read still another. It was the day of Chuck's bankruptcy filing, and his tenants and friends were out in force to protest.

Chuck later blamed the demonstration on Ralph O'Hara. He had obtained a hearing in only three weeks by making a fuss around the Federal Courthouse about the tenants, and a sharp-eared newsman picked up the story. On the morning of the hearing the Detroit paper ran a front-page article on the bankruptcy. The account was factual in reporting Charles Costa's court appearance, the time, the place, but it was emotional in speculating on the "uncertain fate" of Costa's five thousand tenants. The electric company and gas company had served notice that the power was to go off. Everyone, it seemed, would be shut out.

Chuck listened to the radio newscaster's account of the picketers that morning as he drove in from the suburbs for the hearing. The thought of the mob waiting on the street for him almost made him turn back for home, but if not today, he thought, someday soon he would have to face them. Chuck was in no mood to be hassled by a mob, not even a friendly mob. He was tired. He hadn't been sleeping well. Night after night he would awaken dreaming about broken mailboxes, and welfare checks floating away in the air. He would wake up with his stomach in knots, and it would stay bound all day. Chuck hoped that the filing would be the end of it. Then, perhaps, he could relax.

Still, he couldn't help but be vaguely amused by the thought of his tenants picketing for him. There was no illusion why they were doing it. It was their lights that would go out, their radiators that would be cold. Yet here they were, protesting that which they had caused. It was their nonpayments that had brought Chuck down, and now they were demanding that someone, perhaps the all-compassionate city, prop Chuck back up. He remembered that when his son Pepe was two years old, he had flushed his ice cream cone down the toilet, then cried incessantly because it was gone. Chuck thought of the tenants as acting like Pepe, crucifying the inner-city businessmen, then mindlessly protesting when there was no more housing to be had, no more stores to serve them. Only the rip-off artists could survive in such a senseless environment, only the real slumlords could profit. Chuck felt sorry for these people, for the city they were unintentionally destroying, and perhaps sorry for himself. But it would all be over soon, he thought, as he pulled onto Lafayette Boulevard and drove toward the crowd in front of the Federal Building.

Chuck parked his Eldorado across the street from the courthouse, and the crowd rushed out to envelop him, washing out the street they crossed and dispensing with all traffic. Chuck knew all the faces. They were his people and, as senseless as it was, he felt glad to see them.

"We're with you, Mr. Costa. . . ." "Get 'em, Chuck. . . ." "You ain't lettin' them do this, are you, Mr. Costa . . . ?" "Goddamn you, stop pushing. . . ." "Charlie, is this true, really I mean . . . ?" *"Viva* Costa. . . ." Chuck elbowed ahead. The crowd moved with him into the street and toward the steps. He could see Ralph O'Hara and Jo-Jo on the steps and about a dozen uniformed policemen. On the side street Chuck spotted a television crew set up on top of a van, following his motion with the strange cyclopean camera. Chuck walked slowly, stopping occasionally to shake the hand of a tenant he hadn't seen for a while, or some tenant he was especially fond of. When he got to the foot of the steps, there was Susan Stanicki holding a sign that read, "Costa's No Slumlord." He stopped.

"Susan Stanicki, isn't it?" Chuck said. "I don't believe it."

"That I learned my lesson?"

"No, that you're not in jail."

"Probation," Susan said. Someone behind her pushed, and she lurched toward Chuck. He helped her back up. "Mr. Costa, I found out Matty Fuller lied to us, and I'd like to make it up."

"Just don't toss any bombs in the courthouse for me."

"I'm sorry, Mr. Costa," she said. Susan brought her eyes down to the ground.

"We all are, kid," he said as he pushed on up the stairs. He passed the police ring, which sagged under the crowd's motion, and went in.


Peter Balantine wasn't in the crowd that morning. He had read the paper early, and seeing the article, decided this would be the last morning that he could collect rents for Chuck. He'd need the money more than ever now, Peter figured. And if it was the last thing he would do as general manager, it was to collect some of it.

"It's no use," Sheila told him as he dressed to leave. "No one's going to pay when they think they might be out on the street in a few days. They'll be holding onto their money to find another pad."

"That's not right. Costa has treated them well."

"So what? It don't matter how good he's treated them; they've got to look out for themselves, Peter. Collecting ain't wise in your mood."

"You mean street-wise," Peter said. He zipped up his jacket. "And I guess you know enough about streets to be giving me lessons."

She sat down on the couch and looked away from him. "Look," he said, "I didn't mean that. I don't know why I say those things. I'm upset about all of this, and I've got a job to do."

Sheila didn't say anything as he left her.

Peter went straight to the John R. building and right up to Mrs. Brown's door as the first stop in his collecting rounds. Since he had fired the woman as building manager, she hadn't paid a cent in rent. That especially irritated Peter. This corpulent woman had humiliated him; now she was putting him off for rents. The last two times he had asked, she had said she didn't have any money. She hadn't applied for welfare or ADC because it wasn't right, she said, and she'd find another job soon. Peter didn't believe it. He was sure she was pocketing her welfare checks to get back at him for firing her. He was going to collect.

Mrs. Brown answered the door that morning with the newapaper in her hand. She was smiling. "Hello, Mr. Balantine. Martin Luther, Mr. Balantine is here. You put on some coffee water."

"Mrs. Brown, I'm here to collect the back rent," he said. He stepped into the apartment without asking. The television was on. He never remembered being here when it wasn't on and blaring. The boy, Martin Luther, was in the kitchen putting on the water. Peter noticed the rat bite scar on his bare neck and thought back to how Costa had helped this woman get the boy to a physician. "Mr. Costa needs the money, Mrs. Brown. I've got to have it."

"I ain't got no money. I told you that before. I got a chance for a job at the dime store, but that ain't come through yet." Mrs. Brown threw up her hands. "I only wish I had some money."

"You're lying, Mrs. Brown. You people are always lying to me. I'm not going to listen to any more lies. You pay up or get out now."

"Oh, Lord, I ain't got no place to go. Martin Luther, get your stuff. Mr. Balantine is tossing us out in the snow. Where's your brother gone to? Mr. Balantine, I ain't got no place to go."

"Look. All I want is my rent. Just what you owe me." Peter was trying to back off and explain now, but Mrs. Brown was becoming hysterical. "Listen to me, Mrs. Brown, I don't want to put you out."

"Where am I going to go? What am I to do? Get your things, Martin Luther. We're going."

"Mrs. Brown, for Christ's sake, listen to me. If you really don't have the money, you can stay," Peter said. But she kept on babbling, becoming more hysterical by the moment. Peter knew there was only one thing he could do. He slapped her across the face. She stopped in

144

mid-sentence and just stared at him. "That's better," Peter said. Then he noticed Martin Luther standing in his bedroom door pointing a gun at him. He saw the muzzle blast and heard the gun at the same time as he felt the bullet penetrate his left eye.


The bankruptcy filing took only thirty minutes—half an hour to undo the work of ten years. It was like going in for a vasectomy and coming out castrated. Chuck felt as gutted as he knew his buildings would soon be. He sat on a bench outside in the corridor and listened to the footsteps echo off of the marble-sided passageways. Jo-Jo offered Chuck a Chesterfield. He lit up and smiled.

"It's no shame to go bankrupt," Ralph was saying. "Why, some of my clients make a business out of it." But Chuck wasn't listening. He was thinking of the passageway, the echoes. He was thinking of the cigarette in his hand. He was thinking of Jo-Jo sticking by him through a process he was sure the Goliath didn't really comprehend. Chuck was diligently thinking about anything but the bankruptcy filing. He wasn't ready to examine that yet, for he would have to decide what his next step would be, and right now, he had no notion of a direction.

"Mr. Costa?"

Chuck looked up to see John Denise, a radio news reporter. "Not now, John, I'm not in the mood for an interview." Chuck got up and started down the long corridor toward the door. The reporter kept by his side. Jo-Jo and Ralph followed.

"Mr. Costa, who's going to help your tenants now?" the reporter asked. He held a tape recorder microphone up to Chuck as they walked. "Did they decide who was going to take over the apartments? Is the utility company going to shut off the electricity as they threatened? Who's going to help your people relocate?"

Chuck stopped and looked at the reporter, then took the microphone. "In the old country," he said, "we have an expression that if you want to find a helping hand, look to the end of your arm. You tell them that, John. You tell them that so everyone can hear it." Chuck gave the microphone back and stepped out into the crowd that was still gathered on the courthouse steps and sidewalk.

145

"It's all over," Chuck said. "You can all go home now. There's nothing more you can do today." His words, however, were lost in an onrush of people, all trying to get in close and ask Chuck Costa what was happening to them. Chuck couldn't move, so he talked to individuals. He tried to give them a personal comment, to break them out of the crowd. From the back of the crowd he heard Georgie yelling his name and shoving toward him. Chuck pushed toward Georgie's voice. Jo-Jo helped clear the way.

"Chuck," Georgie said. He slipped into the inner circle. "Pete Balantine's been shot."

"Oh, Christ," Chuck whispered, and for a moment felt his legs buckling. "Get out of my way, everyone, let me go."

It took about twenty minutes for Chuck to fight his way out of the crowd and drive to the hospital. On the way, Georgie filled him in on what had happened. Chuck drove with his hands on top of the wheel, a position which kept Peter's diamond ring in front of his view.

The redheaded nurse was again on the desk as he entered. "Well, Mr. Costa," she said, smiling.

"Peter Balantine?" he asked. "How is he?"

"I'm sorry, Mr. Costa, he's dead."

A small gray-haired woman had been sitting in a chair next to the desk, crying into a handkerchief in her lap. A police sergeant stood next to her. It was Mrs. Balantine, and when she heard Costa's name, she got up and came toward him.

"You're the one," she said. "You're the one who killed my boy."

Chuck stared at her, but he could not answer.

"You pulled him into the gutter. He didn't belong with your kind. You killed him. You," she said. The police sergeant pulled Mrs. Balantine away from Chuck and, as he did, he gave Chuck what seemed like a look of indictment.

Chuck walked out of the emergency room and into the circular drive. An ambulance pulled in and backed up to the door. The attendants leaped out, leaving the red ball on top spinning. They carried in two more stretchers, and he heard one of the attendants say something about knife wounds. He began to walk away as another ambulance pulled in. No, Mrs. Balantine, he thought, I didn't kill your son. The city did.

146

# 12

Chuck left his car in the hospital parking lot and walked. He walked down side streets, past boarded-up buildings, past tenement houses where people were yelling at one another, yelling to be heard over the acid-rock music, yelling to be heard over the impersonal and imposing din of the city. Chuck walked with his hands in his coat pockets and his collar turned up against the wind. He knew it was cold; he could feel it on his face and see it in the streets, cold, vacated streets where only an insensitive newspaper tumbled with the wind along the curb. But Chuck didn't feel the cold within him, for there was nothing left inside him to feel with. He couldn't feel guilt for Peter's death or failure for the demise of his business. Perhaps he should, he thought, but vague emotions were not his medium. He dealt in buildings—mortar, wood, and copper tubing. They were the realities, the solids of his internal structure. He dealt in sensations—the pavement so cold that it crackled under his steps, the breath that puffed out before him, the pressure of the diamond ring on his pocketed hand, the ring Peter had given him as payment for his help. These were the things he understood, the things that now tormented him.

Chuck found himself back at his house on Lincoln. He went in and walked through the empty rooms. Everything was now crowded into the

147

new place in the suburbs, all of the furniture and curios that Chuck could visualize as he walked through the vacant rooms. The telephone was ringing in his office. He tried to ignore its echoing sound in the empty house. But it didn't stop ringing, so Chuck went into his office and picked it up.

"Chuck, is that you?"

"Yeah, Ralph, what do you want?"

"I've been trying to get a hold of you for hours. Where have you been?"

"Walking, I guess."

"Look, the phone has been ringing off the hook since this morning here. My secretary hasn't done anything else but answer your calls. Landlords are calling, Chuck. Your friends. They want you to manage buildings for them."

"You've got to be kidding. Why would anyone want to hire the captain of the *Titanic*?"

"Because they know it wasn't your fault. They've got the same problems. They know your reputation."

"I couldn't help them," Chuck said. "I couldn't save my own business; I can't do anything for them. The demolition ball's gonna tear this town down, back to farmland. Damn it, I can't help it."

"But—"

"Come off it. I appreciate what you're trying to do, and what they're doing, too, but I got nothing to sell them. No answers. Tell them to forget it, and I'll see you later."

Chuck hung up the phone. It started ringing immediately again. He sat and watched it ring, listened to the echo the sound made against the walls, but he didn't pick it up. He didn't care. He couldn't care anymore. He sat alone, trying to piece together the series of events that had brought him here. His mind kept wandering back to the farm, to Peter's ring, to Pam's ragged hair. If he knew how to cry, he might have, but instead he sat and listened and wandered through a circus of disjointed thoughts.

After sitting for an immeasurable time, Chuck heard some noise on the front porch. He went into the outer office and looked out the window to see Jo-Jo on the porch. He was painting the front door. Chuck vaguely recalled having asked Jo-Jo to paint the door some weeks ago, but why he had decided that this was the time, in this cold, Chuck couldn't tell. He was going to go out and stop him, but he didn't want to see Jo-Jo; he didn't want to face anyone yet. Chuck walked back into his office and heard a new noise, this time from the backyard. He looked out the back window and saw three men tugging away at his cyclone fence. They had it partially off, rolling it up behind them. Chuck recognized one of the men. It was Raymond, using a crowbar this time to dismantle his property. Sure, Chuck thought, they heard I moved out, and now they're scavenging. Well, let them have it. He noticed Raymond dancing to stay warm as he worked. He saw the smirk on Raymond's face, the same one Chuck had wanted to tear off in the courtroom.

Chuck went back to his desk and sat down. It's crazy, he thought. Jo-Jo painting the front porch while those animals carry away the back fence. Useless. But the more he thought about those three in his backyard, the more he thought about Raymond's smile, the more his stomach churned with rage. I don't care, Chuck said to himself. I don't care. Like hell, I don't care. Chuck ran through the house, threw open the back door, and leaped from the porch onto Raymond's back. Chuck had him face up on the snow, hitting him again and again. He knew the other two men were somewhere close. He didn't care. He couldn't stop hitting Raymond. Someone grabbed Chuck by the hair from behind, and another set of hands was pulling on his shoulder. Chuck felt himself being dragged off of Raymond. He twisted around and kicked one of his attackers. The other smashed Chuck in the face. On his back, Chuck skidded away like a snake, but out of the corner of his eye he could see Raymond starting to get up, and again Chuck forgot about the others and grabbed Raymond by the legs, pulling him down. All three were soon on Chuck. He could feel the blows to his face, his sides, his chest, but as they came down harder, Chuck could feel less and less. It was almost as if they were hitting someone else as Chuck began to lose consciousness. Then Chuck saw the paint fly and Jo-Jo's form as he threw himself on top of the pile. Jo-Jo peeled them off like potato bugs from seedlings, and two of the men lost interest in the fight when, after being tumbled off, they got a look at Jo-Jo coming at them. The third man, Raymond, was probably too dazed by Chuck's blows to run with his friends, so Jo-Jo got in several extra blows before Raymond limped away.

Jo-Jo helped Chuck over to the porch steps. Chuck could feel pain coming back, especially in his sides, and he wondered if there might be some broken ribs in there. He lay back on the steps, and Jo-Jo gave him a Chesterfield. It was the last in the pack. Chuck's mouth was bleeding, and the taste of blood was mingled with that of the smoke. Still, it tasted good. Chuck offered Jo-Jo the cigarette back, then realized it was stained with blood. Jo-Jo looked at the cigarette. He shook his head to refuse it, and Chuck smiled and took it back. You're the only one who doesn't want my blood, Chuck thought, and the thought amused him. He was feeling better. The pain in his flesh had replaced the agony within him, and of the two kinds of pain, Chuck preferred the physical.

He got up after a few minutes and walked out onto Elizabeth Street. Jo-Jo began to follow, but Chuck motioned him back and, with a hand motion, thanked him. Chuck walked down the street, feeling the pain in his side and the cold which was beginning to penetrate him. At Third and Brainard Streets a car pulled up alongside him.

"Hey, Mr. Costa." Chuck looked to see Frank Gottis, one of the tenants from the Charlotte and Third Avenue building, behind the steering wheel of a rusted-out Buick LeSabre.

"Hi, Frank."

"When's Jimmy getting out of the hospital, Mr. Costa? Say, what happened to you anyhow?"

"Nothing Frank. Jimmy should be out in a few days, why?"

"Because he's got my check. He's got everybody's checks. What hospital is he in, so I can go over there and get my money?"

"Detroit General," Chuck said "I'm going there now."

"Get in, I'll take you."

Chuck got in and was immediately struck by the heat and the odor of cheap perfume, probably emanating from an incense dispenser dangling from the rearview mirror. "Why has Jimmy got all your welfare checks?"

"I don't know that he has, but somebody has. Maybe the mailman kept them. Jimmy told us that since the mailboxes were always getting ripped, he would have the mailman bring the checks directly to his apartment, then he'd give them to us. Then the next day he upped and got mugged."

"He what?" Chuck asked. There was something here Chuck suddenly wanted to know more about.

"He got mugged."

"No, I mean what you said before, that Jimmy had the mail, your mail, and everybody's mail delivered to him."

"Hey, we all had to sign cards that Jimmy got from the postman saying that it was all right. Half of us had our checks stole before, so it seemed a lot safer than in the box. You don't think he's getting the checks at the hospital, do you?"

"No," Chuck said, "but he'd know if the post office is holding them. Drive faster, will you? I want to talk to Jimmy, too."

Jimmy's ward was on the fifth floor. Chuck went ahead as Gottis parked the car. Chuck was in a hurry to find out about the misplaced mail. He entered the ward and spotted Jimmy in the fourth bed, sleeping. Chuck shook him to wake him up, and a nurse taking a temperature from an old man two beds away gave him a hard look, as if to say, we don't shake the patients.

"Jimmy, wake up, will you?"

"Oh, hi, Chuck. Shit, I didn't expect you to come. What happened to your face?"

"Jimmy, I want you to tell me about the mail. How did you get it delivered to you instead of the tenants?"

"Christ, I forgot about the mail. Did anybody get it from my room?"

"That's not important. What I want to know is, is it legal for you to accept other people's mail?"

"Sure it is. The mailman said I should do it because all the mailboxes were torn out."

Chuck smiled and sat down on the edge of the bed. "Why didn't I think of that?" he said to himself. "I'm going to use your phone, Jimmy," Chuck said out loud, then picked it up from the stand next to the bed and called Ralph O'Hara.

"Ralph, this is Chuck. Don't throw away those management offers. I think I've got an idea of how to do it."

"That's great. Do what?"

"Collect rents from welfare tenants. All we have to do is get the mail delivered to the managers. That can be done. Jimmy did it. Then when a check comes in, the manager can have the tenant endorse it and hand it

151

over. The manager takes out the rent and hands him the change. It will work, Ralph. I'm sure it will.''

The nurse came down and tapped Chuck on the shoulder. "We don't sit on a patient's bed," she said. Chuck grinned at her and got off.

"But what if they don't want to pay the landlord?" Ralph asked. "I mean, you can't keep their checks from them."

"No, but you can tell them that if they don't want to pay, that you'll hold their checks for the half hour it takes them to clear out of their apartments. They can pick the checks up on the way out the door. They either pay or go, right then."

"That might work. I'm not sure if it's legal though."

"Who gives a damn if it's legal. You tell those landlords that Chuck Costa will manage their buildings for them. You tell them I'll collect, too."

"But what if it doesn't work, Chuck?"

"Then it doesn't work. I'll try something else. You know, I've been thinking about organizing the landlords to protest this thing. I've got a great idea of how to publicize the problem. What I'll do is bring in cows, chickens, and maybe even some sheep and let them graze on those empty lots that used to be homes. Then I'll call the press and all the landlords for a farm-in. That ought to get this stirred up."

"You're soft in the head, Chuck," Ralph said. Chuck could hear the crack of laughter in his voice.

"Maybe I am soft-headed. Peter says I'm soft on the tenants . . ." Chuck stopped himself, realizing again that Peter was gone. "He may have been right."

"You too soft?" Ralph said.

"Funny, ha. You know, that reminds me of hearing that they found Adolph Hitler in Brazil and asked him to come back and take over Germany. And you know what he said? Hitler said, 'OK, I'll do it, but this time, no more Mr. Nice Guy.' "

"Chuck, you're incorrigible."

"Thanks, Ralph. I'll be over later to get those names."

Chuck hung up the phone and slapped Jimmy on the shoulder in a friendly gesture that nearly tossed him out of bed. Then Chuck went out into the hall. He was thinking now of managing other people's buildings and buying up a few of the choice ones as he went along. Perhaps some safe buildings with nothing but retirees, or condominiums in suburbia. His insides were filling back in as he thought ahead. There was a knot yet in his stomach, but it would have to be ignored for now as he moved ahead.

In the lobby Chuck was stunned to see Anita waiting. She was alone on a large stuffed couch; her eyes were puffed red from crying. "What are you doing down here?" he asked.

"I thought I might find you here. I heard about Peter. I'm sorry."

"Yeah," Chuck said. He felt the knot in his stomach tighten."So am I, but you know, 'Nit, I'm not going to let it lick me." Anita threw both arms around Chuck's neck, and they embraced for several minutes. "Say, it's after suppertime, and I'm starved. Let's go home, and you can fix me some nice green bananas." They laughed and started for the door.

"Mr. Costa," a voice called out. Chuck turned to see a frail black woman in a threadbare cotton coat. "Mr. Costa, do you remember me?"

"No. Oh, wait a minute. You're Jessie Thompson's sister, right? Sure, I saw you several times at her apartment. How is Jessie?"

"She's dead. She went yesterday. I'm here to pick up her slippers and stuff," the woman said. She held up a brown paper bag as evidence. "I got all the kids now, Mr. Costa. Jessie's and mine. That's ten altogether."

"I'm sorry, but we've got to be going now."

"But Mr. Costa, I need a place to keep all the kids. Jessie's landlord don't like all them kids in that room, and now we's going to have to move for sure."

"You on ADC?" Chuck asked.

"Yes, sir."

"I'm sorry, but I'm not a landlord anymore," he said. Chuck took Anita by the arm and started to walk away. But then he stopped and looked back at the woman in the cotton coat. Ten kids, he thought. Oh, hell—"Look, you give me your address," Chuck said. "Maybe I can place you tomorrow. I can't promise anything, but I'll try."

153

# Epilogue

Charles Costa was not beaten. After his bankruptcy he worked as a building management consultant and built up his own business again. Today Charles Costa maintains more than four hundred apartments, not in suburbia, but in the bowels of Detroit, a city Federal Bureau of Investigation records show to be the most violent in America. Costa continues to strive for improved low-income housing through an organization that he founded, the Housing Owners of Michigan Exchange (HOME). Among landlords he argues for a code of ethics that may dispel the ''slumlord'' stigma. In government he fights for laws that allow the small businessman freedom to make a reasonable profit and, in so doing, provide better city living for all. And of the slums, Costa argues: ''The answer is not to take the people out of the slums, but to evict the slums from within the people.''